the way
languages

rion Vincent
athfinder 16

Other titles in the Young Pathfinder series:

Leading the way

Co-ordinating primary languages

Young Pathfinder

16

Bernadette Clinton and Marion Vincent

First published 2009 by:
CILT, the National Centre for Languages
111 Westminster Bridge Road
London SE1 7HR

www.cilt.org.uk

Printed in Great Britain by Hobbs the Printers Ltd.

CILT Publications are available from Central Books, 99 Wallis Road, London E9 5LN.
Tel: 0845 458 9910. Fax: 0845 458 9912. Web: **www.centralbooks.com**

Acknowledgements

The authors wish to thank all the teachers who were in the first cohort of the MA module 'Developing Professional Practice through Implementing Primary Languages' for their ideas and suggestions.

Jane Houlston, Oakthorpe; Jo Walker, Grange Park; Jennifer Wedderburn, Prince of Wales; Helen Jeckells, Cuckoo Hall; Laura Yale, Keys Meadow; Caroline Scott, Wilbury; Julie Hinckley, Hazelbury Junior; Sandra Chaaya, Durants Special; Debbie Pyne, Eversley; Sera Kadem, Galliard.

We also want to thank all the teachers, teaching assistants and pupils in Enfield who have participated in the introduction of primary languages since 2003.

» Contents

» Introduction

» Why do we need a book on the role of the primary languages subject leader?

We are living in very exciting times in the world of primary languages where the positive impact on children's learning is being appreciated.

> 'We continually hear the comment that children enjoy their language learning in primary schools. A specifically primary experience of languages is being developed, linking language learning to learning across the curriculum and making good use of resources, of speakers of the language and of excellent programmes of ICT based learning'
>
> (*Languages Review 2007*, p10).

How we manage the introduction of languages throughout Key Stage 2 (KS2) will set the tone for the production of the skilled linguists so fervently identified as a priority in the document *Languages for All: Languages for Life* (2002). Those who are responsible for this in every primary school face a challenging task. It is the aim of this Young Pathfinder to give guidance to those who have this responsibility.

Different titles are given for the person in this role. Some use the term Co-ordinator and others Middle Leader. In this Young Pathfinder the term Subject Leader is used. The authors made the decision to use this term because they feel that it better conveys the scope of the job that needs to be done. They consider that the role involves leadership, not just co-ordination. Staff in schools will be at different phases of their career when they take on this role and will not necessarily be Middle Leaders in the hierarchy of the school.

In 2007, the Training and Development Agency for Schools published a new framework of professional standards for teachers. These standards are designed to define the characteristics of teachers at different stages in their career.

The authors believe that life in school does not necessarily develop in neat stages, however we realise that some primary languages subject leaders may have come into the teaching profession recently. In this case the Professional Teacher Standards (TDA 2007) available from **www.tda.gov.uk** provide a possible professional development path for you.

The authors have drawn widely on their own experiences as practitioners and advisers and on the work carried out with subject leaders across a variety of schools.

It is crucial to the success of the implementation of languages in your school that you provide strong, confident leadership. Research on the generic qualities needed by a good leader has identified the following:
- Commitment
- Energy
- Enthusiasm
- Enterprise
- Responsibility
- Collaboration
- Initiative
- Confidence

Try to be explicit with yourself about the qualities you have and the skills that you may need to develop.

However, in order to implement this change in the curriculum, the active support of the head teacher is essential. Without it you will not be given the freedom to act nor the back up that will be needed. You will have to plan carefully to ensure that you can manage this implementation successfully. The introduction of languages into primary schools will involve changes and will require you to take a leadership role.

Chapter 1 covers the role of the subject leader and gives advice on the first steps to be taken to implement primary languages.

Chapter 2 looks at the ways in which good learning and teaching practice can be achieved. It also discusses the choices of resources and support.

Chapter 3 is concerned with the training and enthusing of all staff. This includes a model of an introductory staff meeting, Teaching Assistant programme and professional development plan.

Chapter 4 deals with planning and writing policies. Medium term planning gives examples of cross-curricular work.

Chapter 5 covers all aspects of monitoring at school and national level, including by OFSTED.

Chapter 6 shows how assessment can be carried out on a day-to-day level, periodically and at transition points.

Chapter 7 Community cohesion through international links promotes local and community involvement.

Chapter 8 looks at transition and transfer between key stages. It includes an example of a KS2/KS3 transfer document.

The authors hope that you will find this book useful and stimulating. It can be a daunting prospect to set out on the road to succeed as a primary languages subject leader. However, the authors hope that you will be shown how you can take steps to achieve all of the Professional Standards for the Excellent Teacher by following the guidance and advice that is given in this book. It is organised in a way that should help you to plan how you will implement and maintain the introduction and embedding of languages into the primary curriculum.

As stated earlier, this is an exciting time to be involved in primary languages. Do make the most of this opportunity for yourself and your pupils. Well done for taking up this challenge. We predict it will be an excellent career move.

Chapter 1
» Getting started

» Being a subject leader

There are specific attributes and skills that every subject leader will need to demonstrate. These are detailed in the Professional Standards for Teachers documentation. They include taking a lead in:
- Planning
- Monitoring
- Delivering
- Team working
- Assessing
- Reviewing and evaluating

A complete list can be found in the Professional Standards for Teachers.

» What is special about being a primary languages subject leader?

Whilst the basic requirements for all subject leaders in every subject will be the same, there are additional aspects of the primary languages subject leader role to be considered.
- You will have to make, or at least be involved in, decisions about which language or languages to teach and the mode of delivery. This level of decision-making is not part of the remit of other subject leaders.
- You will have to match the pupils' needs with the language skills of staff and the overall vision of the school. Your skills in diplomacy may well be called into use.

- You will have to deal with the feelings of some staff, governors and parents of the value of including this subject in the curriculum. There may be concerns about how it will be fitted into a curriculum which already has many established subjects. You will need to involve the whole school in finding opportunities across the curriculum to reinforce language learning.
- It may be necessary to convince many native English speakers of the benefits of modern methods of teaching languages which may be different from their own experiences at school.
- Traditionally, primary teachers were not required to have language teaching skills and so a training programme has to be provided. This will have to be included in your planning over a number of years.
- You may feel uneasy about your own level of expertise and knowledge in the subject. You will need to ensure that your own language skills and teaching methodology develop by taking advantage of training opportunities.
- The development of resources for teaching primary languages is now blossoming and informed choices need to be made about what is appropriate in each school, often without background knowledge in this field being accessible within your school. In most other subjects there will be someone you can turn to who has prior knowledge and experience.
- There may be some experienced teachers who were involved in the pilot scheme to introduce primary French in the 1960s and 1970s and feel concerned about how effective this new initiative will be.
- There may not be a wealth of experience to draw on in the school, whereas in other subjects there is usually expertise available in school.

The diagram on the next page gives an overview of the role of the primary languages subject leader. In this book the authors will address all of these roles/tasks.

» Making decisions about which language or languages

Before you embark on the planning for the teaching of a language or languages you will have to consider a number of factors. These include:
- The current situation in school in relation to language teaching
- The skills and interests of the staff
- The world view of the school
- Existing international links
- Prior linguistic skills of the pupils
- The languages taught by the local secondary schools
- Parental views
- Resources available

Role of the primary languages subject leader

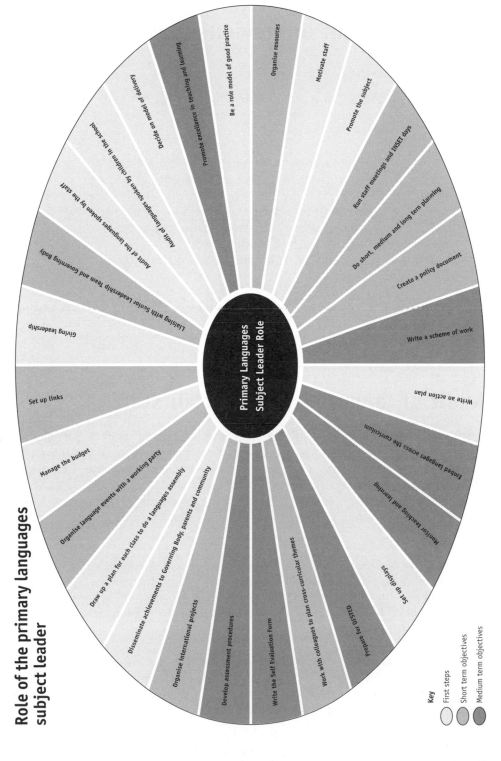

Primary Languages Subject Leader Role

Be a role model of good practice
Organise resources
Motivate staff
Promote the subject
Run staff meetings and INSET days
Do short, medium and long term planning
Create a policy document
Write a scheme of work
Write an action plan
Embed languages across the curriculum
Monitor teaching and learning
Set up displays
Prepare for OFSTED
Work with colleagues to plan cross-curricular themes
Write the Self Evaluation Form
Develop assessment procedures
Organise international projects
Disseminate achievements to Governing Body, parents and community
Draw up a plan for each class to do a languages assembly
Organise language events with a working party
Manage the budget
Set up links
Giving leadership
Liaising with Senior Leadership Team and Governing Body
Audit of the languages spoken by the staff
Audit of languages spoken by children in the school
Decide on model of delivery
Promote excellence in teaching and learning

Key
○ First steps
○ Short term objectives
○ Medium term objectives

» Audit of current or previous practice in your school

You will need to find out what language teaching, if any, has taken place in your school.

Things to consider:
- Is there any language teaching taking place at the present time?
- Have the headteacher/governors/parents any knowledge of language teaching in the past?
- Are there any resources in the school which relate to language teaching?
- Has your Local Authority primary languages adviser any record of involvement in language teaching at your school?
- Is there evidence of planning? If lessons are taking place you will need to arrange to observe some.

With this information to hand, you will have the necessary evidence to support your decisions and planning.

Discuss your findings with your head teacher.

» Audit of language skills for all staff

It is essential that the teaching of languages involves as many staff as possible. An audit of the language skills of your existing staff can take place as an initial exercise to provide information towards the decision making about which language or languages will be taught in your school.

Ask for time at a meeting when all the staff are present to introduce your language survey.

At the meeting explain to colleagues that you will be asking everyone to complete a simple audit of her/his language skills. Make it clear what the purpose of this audit will be and how the information will be used. In this way staff will understand better how their own skills will be valued and feel involved in the planning process for your own school.

An example of an audit is shown in this chapter. The purpose is to identify the individual language experience and skills of staff. Audits identify hidden talents that can then be used for the benefit of the school. For example, in one school the audit showed that a newly qualified teacher had qualifications and expertise in Spanish which she was keen to develop and share and, on that basis, the school chose Spanish as their main language. Audits also enable all staff to develop their expertise and to receive relevant training which can enhance and expand their own linguistic experiences and professional development.

Example of an audit

Languages audit: _____

Name: _____

1. Of which languages, other than English do you have any knowledge?

   _____

   _____

   _____

2. Give some details of your experiences of using languages (for example, grandparents or wider family; living in Somalia; travelling in Greece).

   _____

   _____

   _____

3. Assess your confidence in being able to teach beginning learners on a scale of 1 to 4 where 4 is the highest:

   Language _____ 1 2 3 4

   Language _____ 1 2 3 4

4. Highest level of qualification achieved:

   _____

   _____

   _____

» Possible use of audit information

The use of the audit ensures that no expertise in languages is lost. There are many different ways in which the information can be used, for example:

- Crucially, experts are identified who can support other members of staff in delivering the chosen language(s).
- School-based and external training can be tailored to meet the needs of the staff.
- The main language taught in school can be complemented by staff who are confident in another language which they can teach in addition to the main language
- Breakfast clubs, lunchtime and after school clubs can be run in addition to the main taught language.

The results of the audit will need to be discussed with the Senior Leadership Team and decisions made at that level, taking into account the other factors outlined earlier in this chapter.

Below is an example of how one primary school has used the information from the audit of staff skills to ensure suitable training was received and then to promote a range of language experiences for the pupils. The audit revealed that as well as having a teacher with sufficient expertise to aid teachers in KS2 to deliver French as the main language, other staff members had skills which they were keen to use. The school had a high intake of Turkish children. It was therefore decided to use the Turkish speaking TA to promote the language in the school, raising the self-esteem of the Turkish children. Similarly, the school had a number of Greek children and the involvement of the Greek specialist in the Greek project raised the profile of the language.

Case Study of Churchfield Primary School

This is an example of a school who embraced 'Languages for All'

- French is taught by a primary languages specialist to all classes in Years 3, 4, 5 and 6.
- Turkish is taught to all classes in Year 5 as a foreign language by a Turkish-speaking TA supported by the class teacher. The TA has attended the DCSF Higher level Teaching Assistant/Teaching Assistant course
- Turkish Breakfast Club – is also run by the Turkish-speaking TA.
- Italian lunchtime club is run by a TA who has attended the Teaching Assistant course.
- Spanish lunchtime club is run by a language specialist.
- A Greek specialist worked with the Year 5 teachers for half a term on the Greek history topic.

It can be seen that the language activities came out of the audit of skills because the school was keen that skills are recognised and used.

» Mode of Delivery

You will need to decide which approach to take in delivering languages. The Key Stage 2 Framework for Languages Part 3, Section 1, p2 suggests three models of delivery:

> *'minimum of 60 minutes per week is needed for children to make progress, but this can be spread across the week. A "little and often" approach is ideal as it enables children to recall languages and reinforce their understanding and skills at regular intervals. The time can be organised in different ways, for example:*
>
> *15 minutes per day*
> *3 x 20 minutes*
> *2 x 30 minutes plus one shorter session of 10 minutes'*

Once you have decided on the language or languages to be taught you will need to decide who is going to do the teaching. You may need to have an interim and a longer term plan. Debbie Pyne, one of the participants in the MA module 'Developing Professional Practice through Implementing Primary Languages', has carried out research into the issue of who is the best person to teach languages in primary school.

> *'Whilst specialist teachers have great ideas and excellent language skills, they are unfamiliar with the primary MFL methodology and do not know how to meet the learning styles of primary aged children. There are many advantages to the class teacher delivering the MFL curriculum. The weekly time allocated for MFL can be divided throughout the week. It is believed to be better, for example, to have three 20 minute lessons each week as this reinforces vocabulary in the target language, than a full hour each week. It certainly makes it easier to develop cross-curricular links with MFL. Tierney and Hope, for example, give ideas of how MFL can be used in PE. Finally, class teachers know their pupils so there is less likely to be problems with behaviour management and work can be differentiated to suit all abilities and learning styles within the classroom in order to keep children motivated'.*
>
> (Pyne D. (2007) unpublished MA Module, Middlesex University; MIDWHEB p11).

She goes on to recommend the paper 'Class teacher or language specialist?' one of the Best Practice Guides to be found on the Primary Languages website. However you may be receiving support from a specialist teacher and feel that this is appropriate for your school to support you in the early days. Part of your role as subject leader is to plan for training to enable class teachers to gradually take over the delivery of the new language.

A timetable for the teaching of languages needs to be drawn up so that delivery can be monitored. This can include 5 minute slots each day where, for example, *Take 10 en français* (Devon Education Services) might be used.

» Governors

As soon as you can, arrange to attend a meeting of the Governing Body to present a report on the languages initiative. Ensure that languages are included in the annual plan of presentations and reports to the Curriculum committee of the Governing Body and the full Governing Body meeting. It would be helpful if you were able to identify those governors who have a particular interest in languages. Ask for a 'languages champion' from among the governors to volunteer to keep in touch with the developments in languages in your school and to act as an advocate. Continuity can be provided by the teacher governor, especially if she/he is involved in the teaching of languages.

You should now feel confident to embark on your language journey. With this background knowledge, you need to ensure that you know what the aspects of an excellent primary languages lesson are and how you can be a role model for the rest of the staff.

Chapter 2
» Good practice, resources and support

» Good primary practice

In the *Key Stage 2 Framework for Languages* (KS2 Framework), it states that language learning offers opportunities for children to:

- *gain enjoyment, pride and a sense of achievement;*
- *express themselves creatively and imaginatively in other language;*
- *apply and develop their knowledge of languages and language learning;*
- *explore and apply strategies to improve their learning;*
- *explore their own cultural identities and those of others.*

(Introduction, p5 2005).

This is in line with the Primary Strategy as set out in the document *Excellence and Enjoyment* (DfES/0377/2003) available online at **www.standards.dcsf.gov.uk/primary/publications/literacy/63553**.

In this document it is clearly set out what good learning and teaching should include:
- Ensure every child succeeds.
- Build on what learners already know.
- Make learning vivid and real.
- Make learning an enjoyable and challenging experience.
- Enrich the learning experience.
- Promote assessment for learning.

This approach has been further reinforced by the Every Child Matters agenda (**www.everychildmatters.gov.uk**), launched in 2004, in which the government set out

its aim for every child, whatever their background or circumstances, to have the support they need to:
- be healthy;
- stay safe;
- enjoy and achieve;
- make a positive contribution;
- achieve economic well being.

Good primary language teaching encompasses all the objectives and outcomes from the three documents above. It is important that you as the primary languages subject leader are clear what good primary languages teaching is and what a good lesson looks like. It is important to have a thorough understanding of the Key Stage 2 Framework for languages and how to implement this in school.

The Framework has five strands:
- Oracy (speaking and listening).
- Literacy (reading and writing).
- Intercultural Understanding.
- Knowledge about Language.
- Language Learning Strategies.
- and a primary language learning experience has to include children achieving the objectives in all five.

The five strands should be reflected in the planning, delivery, and outcomes of primary languages and in the work that children produce. However, how will you as the subject leader know what good practice in language learning is and support your staff to develop excellent practice?

» The Primary Languages website

The Primary Languages website has been set up precisely to provide examples of good practice and to give support for developing professional practice. This will key be for you as the subject leader to support your own and your colleagues' teaching through providing relevant resources, information and online guidance. The website is a source of information about what is happening in the primary languages field and gives guidance on good practice, resources and available professional development. It also offers links to websites suitable for use with young learners in a variety of languages, along with access to banks of teacher-made resources and access to the online catalogue where you can search for teaching materials currently held in the CILT library.

The CILT Primary Languages website

The Primary Languages website includes a section called the Training Zone. This is a key professional development resource to illustrate the principles of the KS2 Framework for Languages. It comprises a bank of video clips showing real examples of primary languages lessons and case studies on planning and implementing primary languages. Each clip comes with downloadable audio files and transcripts in 6 different languages and a professional development 'think piece' to explore and develop the key themes.

The Training Zone includes four main sections:
- Leaders' Zone
- Teachers' Zone
- Trainers' Zone
- The Media Library

The Trainers' Zone is for registered trainers on the CILT Training the Trainers programme and those working in initial teacher training institutions.

The authors have found it very useful to use this website in INSET sessions with staff. You, as the subject leader, can use the short video sequences which show, for example, a teacher taking the register or using the foreign language in a PE lesson to demonstrate how every member of staff can give some language input. You can guide your colleagues through the site.

» **Using the Primary Languages Training Zone**

Arrange a session with a group of staff to work with some of the clips on the training zone. For example,

1 **Focus on the theme of Progression**

Click on the Jigsaw activity in French. Explain that this game uses coloured jigsaw pieces which hide pictures on an interactive whiteboard. The aim is to motivate the children to manipulate language and to build longer and more complex sentences in French. The children start by saying '*Je pense qu'il y a ...*' and then incorporate nouns, adjectives and phrases.

Ask your group to suggest the elements which help pupils to make real progress in extending their use of language. You may need to look at the short clip several times. Elements they may mention:

a) Challenge

b) Time limit

c) Realistic communication

d) Elements of surprise

e) Independence and maturity

f) Prompts

You can click on Professional development and print off suggestions for exploration and development. Further ideas are given on links to the Framework, next steps and developments that you as subject leader can make yourself modelling good practice for other members of staff.

2 **Another interesting clip to observe when exploring good elements of learning is the sound-spelling story in German under the theme of 'Using the KS2 Framework'.**

Again ask your group to identify key elements which enable pupils to make the links between sounds and spellings, thus preparing the pupils for independent reading. Your staff may identify:

• How the teacher shows the picture and the written word enabling them to make the sound-spelling link.

• The way in which pupils develop a basic knowledge of the writing system, the spelling and structure of the language.

• How the teacher emphasises certain sound/spelling links important in German, e.g. the 'sh' sound in the 'St' of *Sterne*; 'sh' sound in *spät*; the long 'o' sound in *Mond*.

• How the teacher uses rhythm and clapping out syllables to help with memorisation.

There is a wide range of examples on the website which you can explore to develop a common understanding of good practice.

The authors also refer you to the Enfield website **www.mfl.enfield.lgfl.net** which is continually developing. In the section on Primary Resources the work is organised under language. There is material in French, German, Spanish, Italian, Greek and Turkish.

Our colleagues who teach Turkish have developed their own materials and have been particularly good at producing power point presentations for use on their Interactive Whiteboards. They are happy to share these with others.

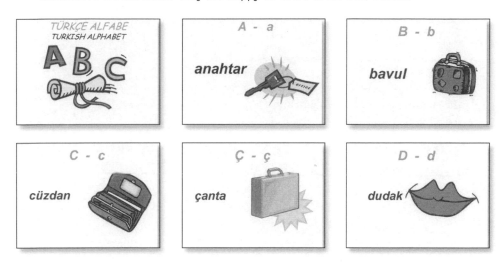

There are comprehensive lists of published resources and classroom materials in *A Flying Start* (YPF11) and *Speak Up!* (YPF15) listed in the Bibliography.

» Choosing Resources

It is impossible to give you one infallible guide for choosing the resources that are right for your school. What you need will depend upon your school's approach to language learning and teaching. We can provide a checklist to assist you in making your decisions. Whilst there are lots of published primary languages resources, you will find that you have a wealth of resources readily available in your school, for example, maths equipment, soft toys and puppets, playground and PE equipment, classroom items, music, globes and world maps, dressing up clothes for role plays.

When buying resources you will need to ensure that you have a variety of materials which support pupil progress in the five strands of the Key Stage 2 Framework; and to support you in delivering your Scheme of Work.

Below is a checklist which you can use to decide which resources are best for you. You may consider that if a resource gets seven ticks in the 'Yes' column then it is worth buying.

	Checklist	Yes	No
1	Does this resource enable teachers to cover the KS2 Framework Objectives?		
2	Does this resource support pupils' progress in oracy, literary, intercultural understanding, knowledge about language and language learning strategies?		
3	Will pupils find it attractive and usable?		
4	Does it include Interactive Whiteboard material which will challenge and engage pupils?		
5	Does it avoid being a type of watered down secondary-style text book?		
6	Do you find it appealing and useful?		
7	Can you see where it will fit into your planning in your Scheme of Work?		
8	Will it provide a stimulus for creative activities such as singing, movement, drama?		
9	Do you feel that non-specialist teachers will be confident to use it?		
10	Does it seem to be a good investment that will not be too dated in a few years' time?		

» Suggested starter pack

You may wish to put together for each teacher starting teaching a language a simple starter pack. Below are suggestions as to what this may contain.

Starter Pack
Soft balls and bean bags
Flashcards with smiley and sad faces; thumbs up and thumbs down etc.
'Traffic lights' for responding in the plenary and for doing peer assessment
Number fans
Coloured cones used in PE
Sponge die
Plastic clocks
Puppets and soft toys
Early Start DVDs (**www.earlystart.co.uk**)
The Language Factory song CDs (**www.language-factory.co.uk**)
List of good free websites
Subscription to atantot (**www.atantot.com**)
A mantra talking pen and greetings poster (**www.mantralingua.com**)

Chapter 3
» Staff development

To support the staff in school to deliver high quality language teaching, as well as keeping yourself up to date and with improved skills, you will need to ensure that support is provided in two key areas:

1 The enhancement of language skills
2 The development of confidence in using language teaching methodology

Whilst these areas will be linked – confident linguists will be more likely to relax and give opportunities for more active learning – it is better to approach them separately, as each will require different support and input.

» Extending your own and your colleagues' language skills

There is a range of courses which can be accessed by your staff to improve their language skills. Many of these take place abroad and are funded through the European Union Comenius programme. Go to **www.britishcouncil.org/comenius** for more details. These are one week or two week language courses which can also include job shadowing in a primary school abroad. CILT also offers week long courses to improve teachers' language and methodology in France, Germany, Italy and Spain.

If staff are not able to go away from home because of family commitments, explore courses nearer home. For example, the Modern Languages Degree Department at Middlesex University runs a three day language course each year for primary teachers. You will receive support with this from your Local Authority adviser or consultant for primary languages or your local specialist language college.

Keep up to date about the linguistic upskilling frameworks produced nationally and how these have been incorporated into your Local Authority

You might also consider grouping together with some other local schools to run twilight language classes. Each term run a series of five or six classes, one hour a week. Do not try to get people to commit to every week of the term as this will prove unsustainable. If possible, get a native speaker to provide a good model of language. For beginners, the framework of the QCA Units 1–12 can be used as the basis of the course. This will then develop language skills within the context of what they will be teaching. Ensure that the sessions are lively and fun and be sensitive to people's lack of confidence in their language skills.

In addition, there are web-based courses that staff can access in their own time. For example, the BBC offers a wide variety. Go to **www.bbc.co.uk/languages** for more information. The Consejería de Educacíon and the Instituto Cervantes offer online Spanish courses. (see **http://ave.cervantes.es** for further information). For German, contact the Goethe Institute at **www.goethe.de** and, for French, contact the French Institute at **www.institut-francais.org.uk**

» **Effective training**

CILT runs some excellent one-day courses on teaching methodology. Go to **www.cilt.org.uk** for further details.

In the DfES document Leading and co-ordinating CDP in Secondary schools (2005) the authors refer to research carried out on teachers' own views of the professional development activities that have had most impact on their own classroom practice. They identified:

> '• *Opportunities to learn from and with other teachers, in their own or other schools.*
> • *Observing colleagues and discussing teaching with them.*
> • *Through working together on real school improvement problems, drawing on best practice.*
> • *Taking part in coaching or mentoring programmes.*
> • *High quality, focused training on specific skill areas, underpinned by excellent teaching materials and direct support to apply learning back in the classroom.'*

> (*Leading and co-ordinating CDP in Secondary schools*, 2005, Section 1, p5)

If these are indeed the most effective methods of improving practice, then they should be incorporated into a training programme for both primary and secondary teachers.

» Modelling and coaching

Coaching is now used throughout the Primary Strategy and is closely linked to the Personalisation agenda. The role of coaching in schools has been boosted by the work on the Key Stage 3 MFL Dissemination and Development programme and much of the approach is also applicable to primary schools. Take a look at the KS3 material on **www.cilt.org.uk/ks3/dissemination/dissemination.htm** for more training ideas.

In their book *Student Achievement Through Staff Development*, Joyce and Showers summarise what they mean by coaching. This is a useful definition to bear in mind when coaching is being talked about so widely.

> 'The coaching relationship is simply a partnership in which two or more people work together to achieve a goal. Visiting one another as they practise, they learn from observing the other person and particularly by watching the students' responses to the cognitive and social tasks that are presented to them. They discuss how to help the students respond more powerfully and how and where to apply their new skills'.
>
> We have many people who believe that the essence of the coaching transaction is in the offering of advice to the partner who is observed. It is not. Each partner learns by watching the transaction. Each teaches by demonstration rather than by criticizing the other person's behaviour. Hence a partnership is forged in the continuing career-long experiment on how to each more effectively.'

(*Student Achievement Through Staff Development*, 1988, p95)

Practically what will this mean for the subject leader? The feedback given by teachers shows that the most effective training is to spend time learning from and team teaching with colleagues. This is a model that has been used in many Local Authorities.

- The class teacher who is new to language teaching is partnered with an experienced linguist, often with a secondary background who is not very familiar with the primary classrooms.
- The two people work together over the course of a year, learning from each other, discussing ways to help pupils to respond more powerfully to the language input.
- The linguist will begin by teaching the class with the class teacher participating.
- The two colleagues will be given time to plan together and to discuss ways to provide better learning opportunities.

- The class teacher will deliver the following lesson to reinforce and extend the learning.
- The outcome will be to produce keen and skilful linguists in a primary context.

This model is very similar to the lesson study approach being highlighted by the Primary Strategy in their 'Improving Schools Programme' (DCSF, 2008). As subject leaders you may not be able to play this role but can support and monitor the process and ensure that the class teacher is equipped to teach by herself/himself the following year.

» Developing the skills and talents of support staff

The staff audit may well have revealed that it is not only the teaching staff who have skills. The expansion in the numbers of Teaching Assistants (TAs) has brought into schools people with a vast range of experiences and skills. Many of these, in some areas of the country, are bilingual and most, therefore, have an understanding of second language acquisition. In 2005 the DfES sponsored a course, piloted in three Local Authorities, as a result of which, it was realised that with appropriate training and support, teaching assistants, higher level teaching assistants and bilingual teaching assistants could make a valuable contribution to the provision of primary languages.

» Teaching assistant course and outcomes

For Teaching Assistants, the course is delivered usually over seven sessions with a contact time of 20 hours. In addition it includes an observation of a primary languages lesson and a lesson delivered by the TA which is observed and feedback is given.

The following elements are included in the course:
- How to carry out a survey of languages spoken in the local school community.
- How to evaluate professional values and practices.
- Sharing of each person's language journey.
- Teaching and Learning including a repertoire of activities; classroom organisation and approaches use of resources and ICT.
- Planning and expectations.
- How to evaluate celebrate and record pupils' progress and achievements.
- Links with TA and HLTA accreditation.
- Career development and support.

Case Study

In Enfield Local Authority there is a course that has been run each year since 2005 to train teaching assistants to support the language learning. Numbers have ranged between 10 and 12. On the 2007 course there were ten teaching assistants. Some were completely bilingual and others had skills in a language which they wanted to use to contribute to the language learning in their schools. They had the following range of languages (some had more than one language):

French	3
Greek	3
Turkish	2
Spanish	3
German	1
Somali	1
Twi	1

Outcomes:
- Two Teaching Assistants started on the Foundation degree, one of whom started working with the Year 3 teacher to implement Spanish;
- Another TA supports the implementation of Spanish into Year 3;
- One continued supporting the French teaching and enrolled on the Graduate Teacher Programme to achieve qualified teaching status;
- One set up a Greek after school club;
- One supported the introduction of Turkish in school and improved her own French by taking part in the 2 week study visit to France;
- One became involved with the class language project and improved her own French by participating in the 2 week study visit to France;
- One TA established a lunchtime Greek club;
- One TA continues to provide the translating and support for parents which she did before the course;
- Another TA was refused leave to stay in the country.

So, largely this is a positive picture, enabling the schools to build their capacity to support language learning by encouraging teaching assistants to support language learning in primary schools.

Contact your own Local Authority or the Training and Development Agency **www.tda.gov.uk** for information on local courses.

» Introductory staff meeting

This meeting will provide you with the opportunity to give a brief introduction to your colleagues about primary languages and to engage them in non-threatening fun activities.

The example scheme shown below has been delivered successfully in over 50 schools.

Aims of the meeting

To introduce all staff to:
- The requirements for teaching languages in primary schools
- The KS2 MFL Framework
- The primary languages website
- Primary language teaching methodology
- Ways of embedding languages across the curriculum
- The languages resources that are in school
- The importance of FUN and the promotion of a love of learning

Suggested programme of the meeting – Beforehand display the language resources you have in school.

3.30 Starter activity: For example 'Alouette' from 'Take 10 en français'. Introduction – hand out to each person an information sheet 'Everything you ever wanted to know about KS2 Languages'. Download this from **www.mfl.enfield.lgfl.net**. Briefly summarise the key points. Ensure that you make it clear that KS1, reception and nursery staff can get involved as well.

3.40 Show the **www.primarylanguages.org.uk** website. Use an example activity to get the staff to join in and to show how supportive the website is for those not too confident of their language skills, for example, days of the week in French with actions. Show the Mantra Lingua Talking Pen in French.

3.50 Sing a song – for example, the Spanish song 'La Bella Durmiente' to demonstrate how languages are taught. (The words can be obtained from the QCA Schemes of Work for French, German and Spanish). Introduce the characters on flashcards, hand them out, discuss what the story might be about, sing the song and staff listen and respond. Then get 'volunteers' to dress up as the characters, sing the song again whilst they act their parts. Get the group to suggest what strategies were used to promote language learning.

4.10 Hand out the Framework Objectives for all the Years 3–6 to pairs. Divide the participants into Year 3, 4, 5, 6 and ask them to look at one year and discuss in groups which Framework Objectives have been touched on in the Bella Durmiente activities. Take feedback from each group.

4.25 Questions and discussion. Finish with a Foundation Stage activity from 'Take 10 en français'.

In the staff meeting there will obviously not be time to address all the advice in depth. More training will need to be given, preferably on an INSET day. Once staff have an overall view of what is involved it will be possible to give ongoing support and advice.

La Bella Durmiente

Resources and props	Words of song in Spanish
Flashcards of:	*Había una princesa, princesa, princesa*
Beautiful Princess	*Había una princesa, princesa*
Young Prince	*Ella era muy hermosa, muy hermosa,*
Witch	*muy hermosa*
Apple	*Ella era muy hermosa, muy hermosa*
100 years	
A spell	*La bruja era muy celosa, muy celosa,*
	Muy celosa
Props:	*La bruja era muy celosa, muy celosa*
crown	
sword	*Le ofreció una manzana, manzana, manzana*
witch's hat	*Le ofreció una manzana, manzana*
wand	*La princesa se durmió, durmió, durmió*
100 year old cloak	*La princesa se durmió durmió*
tiara	
	Pasaron más de cien años, cien años,
	cien años
	Pasaron más de cien años, cien años
	Llegó un joven príncipe, príncipe
	Príncipe
	Llegó un joven príncipe, príncipe
	Encontró a la princesa, princesa,
	Princesa
	Encontró a la princesa, princesa
	El embrujo se rompió, rompió, rompió
	El embrujo se rompió, rompió
	Los jóvenes se casaron, casaron, casaron
	Los jóvenes se casaron, casaron
	Sung to the tune of *'There was a princess long ago'* (To be found in Okki Tokki Onga No 20 and many KS1 music books)

» Enthusing and involving staff

A key part of promoting languages will be to get teachers engaged, motivated and involved. You will need to build the confidence of staff to deliver languages and discuss each person's training needs. The best way to do this is through one-to-one meetings following the initial staff meeting. You will have the results of the language audit as a starting point. Ensure your colleagues feel comfortable raising any fears or concerns. Although the meeting will be informal, it will be helpful to have a check list.

In delivering 5 minute sessions each day/or longer lessons what support would you like?

For example
- Observing colleagues in school or in other schools
- Team teaching
- Taking part in twilight language classes
- Attending overseas language courses
- Attending training courses locally or nationally
- Other – please state

Can you suggest other ways that languages can be embedded across the curriculum?

As part of her research, Julie Hinckley, one of the Enfield subject leaders, involved other teachers in observing her classes and recording their impressions of how pupils reacted to the use of the Interactive Whiteboard activities. She, therefore, gave them the chance to be involved in her research, to observe her teaching and to see the impact on the pupils. It was an excellent way of engaging possibly reluctant members of staff in seeing first hand the benefits of language learning for the pupils. She gave the teachers a role in her work and encouraged them to give her feedback. This was a positive coaching situation where each teacher was able to contribute to a discussion on how to improve the learning environment for the pupils.

Julie also gave questionnaires to the staff who then had the chance to give their honest opinions about the Spanish lessons. An example from a very enthusiastic teacher is shown below.

MFL: Teacher Questionnaire about Spanish Lessons and Spanish Software

1) How do you feel about your class learning Spanish?

   Great! They love learning it and all feel capable because there is no set standard. Just everyone learning at same pace.

2) To what extent is it helpful to have an MFL teacher teaching your class Spanish?

   Using skills learnt to speak Spanish for literacy lessons, especially for those with EAL.

3) Do you feel it is of benefit to you to observe Spanish being taught? If so, in which ways is it beneficial to you?

   I observed every lesson and now with Ms Hinkley's support, I can teach any of my classes simple Spanish.

4) Do you believe your Spanish skills have improved due to observing lessons; if so, to what extent?

   As above, but I am also learning for my own personal benefit.

5) What impact has observing Spanish lessons had on your knowledge of how to teach MFL to children?

   I have begun teaching my own language to children in a similar way, in a similar structure. It's very exciting.

6) How do you think you would feel in having to teach Spanish to your class?

   Great! I'm doing it anyway. May need further training though.

ICT questions

7) Please comment on your pupils' enjoyment of the Spanish games I have used on the Interactive Whiteboard.

   They enjoy them a great deal. They can do them independently and also during golden time.

8) What impact do you think the use of Spanish games on the Interactive Whiteboard have had on your class?

   They are taking more ownership of their own learning and when given the opportunity, they will choose to go on a Spanish game.

They are taking more ownership of their own learning and when given the opportunity, they will choose to go on a Spanish game.

As well as encouraging staff to attend language courses abroad, Julie ran regular sessions in school showing them good Interactive Whiteboard resources that they could use, especially useful for those who felt uncertain of their own level of expertise.

In a school which has a wide range of international visits and is beginning to embed the International Dimension into the curriculum, there will be a lot of opportunities to send reluctant teachers on such visits to enable them to see the importance of language learning and to reflect on their own practice as a result of looking at different school systems. Further details are given in Chapter 7.

In another school, a whole school focus for one week on 'Speaking and Listening' involved all staff in using and promoting French as a major contribution to developing pupils' speaking and listening skills.

Where a teacher still feels unable to participate despite all the help you have given, you may need to call on the support of the Senior Leadership Team to find a way to resolve differences. If your school has the policy that all staff will be involved in promoting languages, even if just a few minutes a day, then ways need to be found to bring the particular teacher on board. These can be used as part of an ongoing training programme.

» Professional development plan

Opposite is an example of a training plan, following discussions with individual leaders. A real plan would have to include explicit detail. For example, courses would be named, the amount of money involved for course fees, supply cover dates given for time and release.

Objective 1: To improve the skills of the staff

Activities	Success criteria	Monitoring and Evaluation	Who is responsible	Resources	Deadline	Review date
Twilight language classes	Attendance by 25% of staff and increased confidence	Regular evaluation forms; evaluation of lesson involvement; lesson observation	Languages Subject Leader	Paying teacher; delivering class; time	End of school year	Termly
Attend language courses	Attendance by two staff at national or international courses e.g., CILT courses with EU or British Council funding	By evaluation and feedback from courses and monitoring impact in classroom	Language Subject Leader and CPD Coordinator	Course fees; supply cover	End of school year	Termly
Team teaching and coaching	Regular team teaching and coaching events; growth in confidence	Lesson observation and feedback	Head teacher and Language Subject Leader	Time and release	End of school year	Termly

Objective 2: To enhance staff understanding and delivery of language teaching and methodology.

Activities	Success criteria	Monitoring and Evaluation	Who is responsible	Resources	Deadline	Review date
Staff meetings	All staff understood the approach and feel confident to contribute to language teaching	Audits of Practice; evaluation forms	Language Subject Leader	Time: props	End of school year	Termly
Attend appropriate course	Attendance by 2 staff on Teaching and Learning courses	Feedback given by member of staff	Language Subject Leader	Time: course fees; supply cover	End of school year	Termly
Buy all CILT Young Pathfinder books and maintain a library including useful journals	Staff borrow books, comment on and incorporate ideas into own teaching	Record of borrowing lesson observation	Language Subject Leader	Money for books	End of school year	Termly
Peer observation to share good practice	Regular lesson observation by staff takes place and is timetabled	Records of lesson observation; discussions in and out of meetings	Language Subject Leader	Release time	End of school year	Termly
Observation of KS3 lessons	Year 6 teachers see Yr 7 lessons and learn from practice	Head Teacher and Language Subject Leader to read observation forms; regular report backs	Head Teacher	Release time	End of school year	Termly

Objective 3: To encourage staff to develop further including possibly credit-bearing courses

Activities	Success criteria	Monitoring and Evaluation	Who is responsible	Resources	Deadline	Review date
Send TAs on MFL/TA course as part of their career development	The role of the TAs in school is enhanced through involvement with language teaching	Record of attendance: Post course meeting and planning	CPD Co-ordinator, Head teacher and Subject Leader	Course fees; Release time	End of school year	Termly
Encourage staff to apply to be Leading Teachers	Excellent staff who play a role outside their own school	Lesson observation; liaison with the Local Authority	Head teacher	Release time	End of school year	Termly
Investigate opportunities for staff to gain credits for their work	Staff enrol on credit bearing or career development courses	Monitor courses involved in; keep INSET record; ensure each person on course has a school mentor	Head teacher/CPD Co-ordinator	Funding towards fees	End of school year	Termly

» Classroom based research and gaining credits

As you carry out your subject leader duties, there will have been opportunities to extend your own professional development more formally. You will have been involved in implementing a new initiative; managing change and dealing with the disruption to relationships involved in such changes; and in ensuring that you and the staff at your school can develop the necessary teaching and language skills. This process can go unrecorded and uncredited, or it can be recognised through the achievement of credits as Master's level. There is an MA module called *'Developing Professional Practice through Implementing Primary Languages'* which has been pioneered by Middlesex University through a partnership programme with the surrounding Local Authorities under the heading of MIDWHEB. In the first year, a group of ten coordinators from Enfield enrolled on the module and it ran as a taught course based at the Local Professional Development Centre. However, it can also be adapted to run as an online course with only minimal face-to-face contact. Look at the website **www.midwheb.org.uk** for further details.

The teachers in the first cohort all visited Beijing on a Teacher International Professional Development study visit to look at primary languages teaching. From this visit each person chose an area that she would like to research in her own classroom to improve her own practice. The topics chosen included:
- to investigate the use of the Interactive Whiteboard in primary language teaching and its impact on pupil motivation and learning;
- to investigate the use of movement in lessons to enhance children's learning and enjoyment;
- to research strategies to help develop memory;
- to explore the impact of learning a language on those pupils who have English as an additional language;
- to look into ways that Year 6 teachers can gain the confidence and the skills to happily deliver language lessons.

Each teacher submitted a portfolio for assessment to achieve 60 credits towards an MA that is one third of the final qualification. Each researcher has a school-based mentor who acts as an advocate for them, ensuring that they are given the support they need and that their findings are brought to the attention of the school leadership.

Chapter 4
» Planning and policy

As with other subjects, you will have to ensure that careful, detailed planning is in place for primary language lessons to support teachers in their delivery. The planning will also ensure that bodies such as the senior leadership teams, governors, inspectors and parents have access to the content of the lessons. The school scheme of work and the language policy will contribute to the school development planning.

Using the QCA Schemes of Work and the KS2 Framework

The Key Stage 2 Framework for Languages has been written to provide support for primary teachers in designing their own learning activities. It is 'a core document, offering a practical reference tool for planning, teaching and monitoring the learning process'.

> 'The framework is content free and should be seen as a support,
> not a constraint; a climbing frame, not a cage.'
>
> (*Key Stage 2 Framework for Languages 2005*, Part 1, pp3–4)

In this section the authors aim to show how the five strands of the KS2 Framework:
- Oracy
- Literacy
- Intercultural Understanding
- Knowledge about Language
- Language Learning Strategies

can deliver all the elements of good learning and teaching referred to in the Primary Strategy and in Chapter 2 of this book.

You will need to understand how the strands all fit together and ensure that your children will be receiving an exciting language learning experience. It is also vital that you are able to demonstrate to colleagues how they are able to contribute to the pupils' language learning by working with the five strands and incorporating the teachers' knowledge of primary pedagogy and the primary curriculum.

In Part 2 of the Framework targeted advice is given for different users. Part 3 is a vital tool in the planning and suggests ways in which languages can be embedded in the curriculum.

It also addresses other problematic areas such as mixed-aged classes, small schools, and transition into Key Stage 3.

It is intended that schools use the Framework 'creatively' to provide a framework for long term, medium and short term planning. It challenges teachers to devise their own programmes of work and activities which will 'engage, excite and challenge' the children. If you do not already have a copy of the framework you can order one from: **www.teachernet.gov.uk/publications**.

The QCA Scheme of Work is seen as a comprehensive and stimulating basis for planning the teaching of languages and acts as the long term plan. It is closely allied to the KS2 Framework and reference is made to the strands of the Framework in the Learning Objectives. The scheme of work emphasises the importance of linking the learning to other curriculum subjects. There are six units for each year group: Year 3, Units 1–6; Year 4, units 7–12; Year 5, units 13–18 and Year 6, units 19–24, and there is progression built into the units over the course of the four years. Where a unit corresponds to an activity that takes place in another area of the curriculum, the order of the units could be changed as long as you take into account the prior language for each unit and incorporate any new key language into the unit you would like to deliver.

The individual units provide the medium term plans. These plans identify learning objectives and outcomes and suggest activities to meet these. The sections within each unit are the basis for short-term plans.

» Embedding languages across the Curriculum

The teaching of languages should not be seen as something that is separate from the rest of the curriculum. The advantages of a cross curricular approaches were referred to in the DfEE publication *'All Our Futures'*.

> *'There is considerable overlap and potential synergy between different curriculum areas ... Not least there are similarities in the processes of teaching and learning.'*

*'Creative insights often occur when new connections are made
between ideas or experiences that were not previously related'.*

1999, p88

In Part 3, Section 1 of the *Framework for Languages* the importance of taking opportunities to link languages with other subject areas is highlighted.

*'Time for discrete language work may be needed, but linking
work in languages to other subjects is motivating and effective,
as it provides a real purpose for learning, in a familiar subject.
It is beneficial to use a cross curricular approach to teach
languages'.*

*By integrating languages into everyday classroom work and
routines you will be able to maximise exposure to the language
and make it relevant to the children".*

2005, p2

The Framework for Languages is a very useful planning tool. In Section 3 of Part 3 specific advice is given on:
- Links between subjects;
- Integrating languages with the rest of the curriculum;
- Cross curricular planning using the learning objectives;
- Building languages into a curricular plan for another subject.

The authors suggest ways in which the link with other subjects can be achieved. The ideas show how subject leaders in a range of subjects could work together to bring about the breadth and balance needed in the curriculum which is high on the School Improvement Partnership as well as the OFSTED agenda.

Below are examples of planning sheets which show how delivery of the language learning, using the QCA scheme, can be achieved by links to other areas of the curriculum. The first example is based on Unit 1 *Moi/Alles über mich/Yo*. These are suggested lesson plans for one week's work to be delivered across the curriculum. The second example is based on Unit 6 French *Ça Pousse/Es wächst/Cultivando unas cosas* and provides a strong link with the Science curriculum. Importance is placed on the daily follow-up activities which reinforce previous learning.

Learning Objectives Citizenship and PHSEE Geography	Learning Outcomes	Language Structures New vocabulary and key questions	Phonic Focus	Activities	Resources
Citizenship and PHSEE lesson To raise awareness of languages spoken by the pupils at home and in the classroom (IU.3.2) To recognise that many languages are spoken in the UK and across the world (KAL) To practice new language with a friend in the classroom (LLS) To listen attentively and understand classroom language (03.4)	Understanding and awareness of the linguistic diversity of the class Pupils can produce simple role plays Pupils can give simple greetings to each other on a daily basis and in a variety of languages	In the different languages: What is your name? My name is ..... Hello Goodbye	Children work in small groups with one pupil as teacher who introduces their language to the others focusing on the basic greetings After practicing for ten minutes the groups present what they have learnt to the class in simple role plays Create a graph of the languages spoken		
Geography lesson To locate countries where the French language is spoken (IU3.2)	Understand that French is spoken in countries other than France	In which countries is French spoken?		On a map of the world create a display of countries where French is spoken	Map of the world Globe A range of puppets/ soft toys
French lessons To recognise and respond to sound patterns and words (03.2) To perform simple communicative tasks using single words, phrases and short sentences (03.3) To ask about and express feelings (03.4)	To know that French children often shake hands when greeting each other and use the familiar term 'Salut' with friends Pupils can say 'Bonjour' and 'Salut' with the correct pronunciation Children know how to say 'Au revoir' at the end of the lesson	*'Bonjour!'* *'Salut!'* *'Au revoir'* *'Ça va?'* *'Ça va bien .. et toi?'*	on, j as in *'Bonjour'* u as in *'Salut'*	Children make flag for each country and display on a map Children greet each other moving around the class, saying 'Salut' and shaking hands In pairs, children use puppets to greet each other and say goodbye Practise the sounds 'on' and 'j' and 'u'.	Video of native speakers saying greetings Ball Bean bags Puppets

To respond to the question 'How are you?' with an appropriate answer

Teacher mouths the new words and children guess the word

Introduce the question 'Ça va?'

Hold up thumb for reply 'Ça va bien'

Throw a ball to individual children and ask 'Ça va?' to elicit the response 'Ça va bien'

Use puppets for role plays to include greetings 'Bonjour', 'Salut', 'Au revoir' and 'Ça va?' with the response "Ça va bien'

Daily follow-up activities: Children greet each other in the different language. Pupil 'teachers' lead the activity. Teacher greets and dismisses the class using 'Bonjour' and 'Au revoir'. Children encouraged to greet each other using 'Salut'. Individual children ask members of the class 'Ça va.'.

Assessment Opportunities: Which children an act confidently as teachers? Which children are able to take part in the role play repeating new language? Which children are confident in practicing new language in front of the class and taking part in role plays?

Framework Objectives	Learning Outcomes	Language Structures, New Vocabulary and Key Questions	Phonic Focus	Activities	Resources
Unit 6 Ça pousse					
Perform simple communicative tasks using single words (O3.3)	Children know and say the name of vegetables	'Qu'est-ce que c'est?' 'Un haricot' 'Un petit pois' 'Une carotte'		Show the vegetable to the children, say the name and ask them to repeat it	Pictures of vegetables or real objects
Recognise some familiar words in written form (L.3.1)	Read familiar words aloud	'Une pomme de terre' 'Un oignon' 'Une tomate' 'Un chou'		Use interactive whiteboard to play 'Qu'est-ce qui manque?' What is missing?	
Use the context of what they see/hear to determine some of the meaning (LLS4)		'Choisissez un légume'		Show the children the words 'carotte, oignon, tomate, petit pois'. Discuss possible meanings and differences in spelling between French and English. Introduce remaining words one at a time and match to vegetables.	
Notice the spelling of familiar words (KAL7)				Give the name cards to individual children. Ask them to stand in line putting the vegetables in alphabetical order	
Literacy **Link with Year 3** **Literacy Unit 1 Poetry**				Place digital images of the vegetables around the room. The children choose to stand by one of the vegetables. Those children standing by that vegetable sit down. The game continues until there is a winner.	
Listen to and respond to simple rhymes (O3.1)	Children will know the life-cycle of a plant through learning a rhyme	'Voici une graine' C'est la graine d'une tomate/ d'un petit pois/d'une carotte		Show the children a bean seed and say 'Voici une graine'. Ask questions (e.g., 'C'est la graine d'une tomate? Oui ou non?' to enable children to identify the seed	
Recognise some familiar words in written form (L.3.1)	Recognise similarities and differences in spelling and sound	C'est la graine d'un haricot			
	Present to an audience a rhyme learned by heart	'Voici une graine: Here is a seed La racine pousse: The root grows Après la racine, la tige pousse: After the root, the stalk grows		Present the rhyme aurally using MS Powerpoint ® to see it growing	
Linguistic activities		Après la tige, les feuilles poussent: After the stalk, the leaves grow	Très Après Graine J'aime	Show the children the words for the parts of the plant	
Recognise and respond to sound patterns (O3.2)	Children can recognise the sound made by è and ai			In groups, listen and put lines in the correct order	

Science at Key Stage 2 **Link with Unit 3B:** **Helping plants grow well** **Section 7 Water and plants** To perform simple communicative tasks (O3.3) Experiment with the writing of simple words (L3.3)	Children know how to: Use simple apparatus to measure and record the height of the bean plant Understand that plants need water, but not unlimited water, for healthy growth Know how to record measurements	*Après les feuilles, la fleur pousse:* After the leaves, the flower grows *Après la fleur, le fruit pousse:* After the flower, the fruit grows *La fruit donne les grains:* The fruit gives seeds *Voici une graine:* Here is a seed *Il faut combien d'eau?* How much water is needed? *L'haricot mesure … cm* The bean measures … cm *Une règle: a ruler* *Centilitre: centilitre* *Jour: day* *Date: date* Numbers to 30: *Cinquante: 50* *J'ai utilisé … centilitres chaque fois:* I used … centilitres each time *L'haricot pousse/ne pousse pas:* The bean is/is not growing	Ask the children to create and mime or gesture to illustrate each stage. Children repeat the words of the rhyme with the appropriate mime or gesture Learn by heart and present to an audience Teacher reads a list of words e.g. *feuille, graine, tige, racine, très, j'aime, fruit, tomate, après* Children make a slash through the air when they hear the è sound. Can they work out the two ways of writing the sound (è and ai) Remind the children that plants need water and ask whether the amount of water given will affect the growth Show the children the bean seedlings and ask them how they could be used to investigate the question Children decide what evidence to collect Different groups give a different volume of water each day e.g., no water, 5cm3, 20 cm3 or 50 cm3 Make a chart to record the date, height, volume of water given every two days, e.g. Date: L'haricot mesure … centilitres Date: The bean measures … centilitres Children compare and record findings

Daily follow-up activities: Different children match the names to the vegetables round the classroom. Teacher mouths different lines of the rhyme for the children to guess. The class practises the rhyme. Can the children carry out the measuring tasks?

Assessment Opportunities: Can each child recognise and say the names of the vegetables? Which children are able to remember the lines of the rhyme? Can each child organise the recording of the experiment and report findings to the class?

» Daily activities where languages can be reinforced

The examples are given in French. These are common classroom situations where languages can be used on a regular basis. Use of mime, with arms, legs and facial expressions is most effective!

- Instructions on arriving at the classroom and for moving from one place to another: *entrez, allez-y!, on y va!*
- Greetings between teacher and pupils and between friends: *bonjour* (to teachers), *salut* (to friends), *au revoir, Monsieur/Madame/Mademoiselle.*
- More greetings as the children settle down: *Comment ça va?* Replies: *Ça va bien merci, comme ci comme ça, ça va mal.*
- Forms of politeness: *s'il vous plait, merci.*
- Ways of getting attention: *silence, taisez-vous* (see also below for useful rhymes).
- General instructions to one or more pupils: *en rang (mettez-vous en rang), entre/entrez, assieds-toi/asseyez-vous/lève-toi. Levez-vous, répète/répétez, ouvre/ouvrez, ferme/fermez, écoute/écoutez, regarde/regardez, lève/levez le doigt, lis/lisez, écris/écrivez.*
- Making apologies: *excusez-moi, pardon.*
- Taking the register: Teacher: *je fais l'appel.* Pupils reply: *présent* (m), *présente* (f), *absent* (m), *absente* (f).
- Taking the dinner register: *sandwichs ou cantine?*
- Writing/saying the date using the following displays in the classroom
  a) Numbers 1–31
  b) Days of the week: *lundi, mardi, mercredi, jeudi, vendredi, samedi, dimanche*
  c) Months of the year: *janvier, février, mars, avril, mai, juin, juillet, août, septembre, octobre, novembre, décembre.*
     e.g. *Quelle est la date aujourd'hui? C'est vendredi quinze janvier*
- Celebration of birthdays: *Joyeux Anniversaire, Mon anniversaire est le (deux juillet).*
- Questions/instructions used in connection with labels around the classroom: *qu'est-ce-que c'est?, ou est?, donnez moi.*
- Use of colours in labelling tables, forming groups for indoor and outdoor activities: *blanc, noir, rouge, vert, blue, jaune, marron, violet, orange, gris, rose.*
- Giving praise: *formidable, magnifique, super, bravo, fantastique, merveilleux*
- Mental maths activities: *plus* (plus), *moins* (minus), *fois* (multiplied by), *égalent.*

These rhymes are useful in giving instructions to the class:

a) *Ecoutez*   hands behind ears
    Regardez   hands on forehead 'looking'
    Taisez-vous   finger to lips
    Chut!   finger to lips
    Chut!   finger to lips

b) *Asseyez-vous correctement!*   Sit up straight!
    Levez le doigt!   Hand in the air!
    Croisez les bras!   Fold arms!
    Fermez les yeux!   Eyes shut!
    Ouvrez les yeux!   Eyes open!

c) Sung to the tune of *'Three Blind Mice'*
    Ecoutez, ecoutez,   Hands behind ears
    Regardez, regardez,   Hands on forehead looking
    Asseyez vous correctement,   Sit up properly
    Asseyez vous correctement,   Sit up properly
    Taisez-vous!   Be quiet!

d) Instructions for lining up (Sung to the tune of *'The Farmer's in his den'*):
    Mettez-vous en rang,   Line up
    Mettez-vous en rang,
    Tous les enfants de la classe,   Everyone
    Mettez-vous en rang   Line up

Languages development plan

It is important that you identify the priorities for language teaching in the development plan. In this way you will be fulfilling the part in your role concerning strategic development which OFSTED sometimes asks about. You will need to add detailed planning. The following are suggested headings:

- Objective
- Activity
- Resources
- Who is responsible
- Outcome
- Review date
- Deadline

Any support for teachers delivering the language teaching needs to be clearly assessed, organised and managed by you as subject leader. You will need to ensure that staff skills will be extended to ensure competent delivery of the programme of learning.

The following is an extract from the plan of Galliard Primary School, Enfield Local Authority.

Objective	Activity	Who is responsible	How	Disseminate	Assessment	Outcomes	Review	Date
To ensure the gradual development of the teaching of MFL to all Key Stage 2 children	Year 3 to continue with German lessons and carry through into year 4 Year 3 in Sep to begin on weekly basis	MFL Co-ordinator and B. Clinton	Teacher of German and French (provided by B. Clinton)	MFL Co-ordinator and M. Pattison	Language lessons to be observed and discussions with class teachers about effectiveness of lessons	Children to be actively involved in MFL lessons Current yr 3 to continue with German Classes starting yr 3 from here onwards to commence French lessons	Sep 2005 Sep 2006	Apr 2006 Apr 2007 Jul 2006
To celebrate work on languages throughout the school	MFL Co-ordinator to make display of work carried out throughout the school	MFL Co-ordinator	Work from children on languages practised every half term	Report to Governors	Governors evaluate success of programme from report	Interactive languages display showing work covered throughout the school and children's achievements	Jul 2006	Jul 2006
	Year 3 assembly on work done in German lessons and/or Yr 4 assembly on work done on Italian through Comenius project	Year 3 and 4 teachers	Photos and videos of activities and assemblies	Class teachers	Verbal feedback	Assemblies to highlight work covered in class	Jul 2006	Jul 2006

Further school plans can be accessed on Enfield's website: **www.mfl.enfield.lgfl.net**

» School Languages Policy

Once the initial decisions have been made you will need to draw up a school language policy setting out the vision of the school in the teaching of languages and the school's approach to teaching as there is no prescribed model. You will also need to include the rationale for the language which you have chosen.

The school languages policy should include the following areas:

Aims and Objectives:
- **Context** – your school context and language groups within your school.
- **Vision** – what does your school have to achieve?
- **Organisation** – which language(s), when, taught by whom?
- **Management and Training** – how will the subject be managed? What will you do to sustain and develop the language skills of your staff?
- **The Curriculum** – what planning formats, resources and materials will you use?
- **Teaching and Learning styles** – describe your methods to promote active learning of languages.
- **Assessment** – the Local Authority requires a summative report on every Year 6 pupil to assist with transition; what other forms of ongoing assessment will you use?
- **Monitoring** – who will monitor the quality of learning? How often? Who will train those doing the monitoring?
- **Continuing Personal Development** – CPD

An extract from Eversley Primary School's policy is included. The section on Teaching and Learning in particular shows the positive approach to language learning. Obviously these plans are evolving as experience develops. Each school will need to decide on their own aims and vision.

Aims and objectives

The aims and objectives of learning a modern foreign language in primary school are:
- To foster an interest in learning other languages.
- To introduce young children to another language in a way that is enjoyable and fun.
- To make young children aware that language has structure and that the structure offers from one language to another.
- To help children develop their awareness of cultural differences in other countries.
- To develop their speaking and listening skills.
- To lay the foundation for future study.

Organisation

We teach a foreign language to children in Years 5 and 6 for 30 minutes a week. A specialist French teacher teaches these lessons. The class teacher works alongside.

In addition, the school hosts a privately run after school French club once a week. Classes are open to children in Key Stage 2 and a termly fee is payable.

There is also a lunchtime French club run by a class teacher, open to Years 1, 2, 3 and 4 children on a termly rota and a lunchtime Spanish club.

Teaching and Learning

We use a variety of techniques to encourage the children to have an active engagement in the modern foreign language; these include games, role play and songs (particularly action songs) and use of puppets and soft toys to demonstrate the foreign language. We frequently use mime to accompany new vocabulary in the foreign language, as this serves to demonstrate the foreign language without the need for translation. We emphasise the listening and speaking skills over the reading and writing skills. We also use a multi-sensory and kinaesthetic approach to teaching ie. we try to introduce a physical element into some of the games, as we believe that this serves to reinforce memory. We make the lessons as entertaining as possible, as we realise that this approach serves to develop a positive attitude in the children to the learning of modern foreign languages. We build children's confidence through constant praise for any contribution they make in the foreign language, however tentative.

(full version on **www.mfl.enfield.lgfl.net**)

Chapter 5
» Monitoring primary languages

As part of the school self evaluation process you will need to make a judgement about how well languages are being implemented and, above all, what impact this is having on pupil learning and achievement. The four-point scale used to grade a school's work is:

Grade 1: Outstanding
Grade 2: Good
Grade 3: Satisfactory
Grade 4: Inadequate

» Self Evaluation Form

There is no perfect Self Evaluation Form (SEF), but key features of a good SEF are:
- Details of key strengths and weaknesses so do not dwell on the unremarkable.
- What is special about your subject?
- Good presentation, clarity of thought.
- Evidence of self-evaluation activity.
- Convincing grade-to-text match with evaluative judgements to fit the overall grade, for example, a grade 3 would be evidenced by a majority of 'sound', 'satisfactory', 'average' and 'adequate' judgements.
- Care in the analysis and evaluation of data and performance.
- Presentation and the inclusion of evidence to support views.
- Demonstrate that you have used data which is not in the public domain, for example, informal assessments, class records of grades and show what action you have taken as a result of your analysis.

You will be concerned to comment on languages in the following sections of the SEF:

Section 3: Achievement and Standards
Section 4: Personal Development and Well-Being
Section 5: The Quality of Provision
Section 6: Leadership and Management
Section 7: Overall Effectiveness and Efficiency

Below are examples of ways that you could approach this task. Once again bear in mind that these may appear daunting at first glance. However this is a process which will take time to embed and it may be helpful to incorporate some of the suggestions below into your professional development plans and language development plans.

Section 3: Achievement and Standards

Key Question	Evidence	Comments
How well do our children, of all abilities and backgrounds, achieve?	Pupil progress is tracked from Year 3–Year 6 and records kept.	
	Targets are set and reviewed with pupils.	
	Pupils are interviewed and can talk confidently about what and how they are learning.	
	The majority of Year 6 pupils achieve grade 3 according to the Languages Ladder, the nationally expected level after 4 years of language learning.	
	Lesson observations show appropriate differentiation.	
	Work scrutinies are carried out in each year.	
	Teacher, peer and self assessment data is kept.	

Section 4: Personal Development and Well Being

Key Question	Evidence	Comments
Are our pupils interested in their work, able to sustain concentration and able to demonstrate growing independence?	Pupils are actively engaged and show interest and commitment.	
	Pupils take responsibility for independent research and develop their own learning strategies.	
	Pupils sustain their efforts and manage their time well to complete tasks.	
Do pupils behave appropriately?	Pupils are praised regularly and good behaviour is reinforced.	
	Prompt action is taken to address poor behaviour.	
	Pupils know that their contribution to lesson is valued.	
	Pupils are interviewed and can talk confidently about what and how they are learning.	
Do pupils understand that they are part of a global community where differences and similarities are to be valued?	The Intercultural Understanding objectives are covered well and embedded into a variety of curriculum areas.	
	Languages contribute to the setting up of school links.	
	Languages play a large role in supporting the work for the International School Award.	
	Language learning contributes to the community cohesion requirements at the school, local community, national community and international community levels.	

Section 5: The Quality of Provision
5a: The quality of teaching and learning

Key Question	Evidence	Comments
How well does the teaching and learning ensure that all pupils learn and make progress?	There is a timetable and framework for monitoring the teaching.	
	Lesson observation reports show appropriate differentiation, pace, behaviour management, enjoyment, engagement.	
	Analysis from scrutiny of work.	
	Feedback from pupils, parents and support staff.	
	Evidence of external monitoring and support.	
	Summative assessment reports.	
	Formative assessment reports.	
	Pupils' self assessment showing that they recognise what is good about their work and how to improve.	
	Pupil involvement in planning, delivery and learning shown in documentation and records of discussions in lessons.	
	Individual, group and cohort target setting with clear steps to improve work.	
	Planning for inclusion, especially for most challenging and talented linguists.	
	Audit of the quality of the subject knowledge of teaching staff and of appropriate methodology.	
	All 5 strands of the Key Stage 2 Framework for Languages are being addressed.	

5b: The curriculum and other activities

The following documents need to be produced as evidence of the quality of provision. Check that you have them all, or if not, then a timetable to produce them. They should be kept in a subject leader file.

Curriculum and other activities	Produced ✓
Curriculum Policy statement	
Evidence of how the curriculum is structured.	
Curriculum balance, timetable allocation.	
Inclusion for identified groups.	
Statutory requirements met.	
Extracurricular activities.	
Community involvement through visits and visitors.	
Home/school links including homework.	
Scheme of work.	
Enhancement through working with other schools and partners.	
Evidence of international work, including the ISA.	
Surveys and evaluations by pupils, parents and staff.	
Lesson observation reports.	

5c: Guidance and support for learners

Key Question	Evidence	Comments
Do the pupils understand what they are doing, how they have done and how they might improve?	There are individual support programmes for pupils at either end of the spectrum of ability in languages.	
	Pupils can talk about how they can develop and improve their work.	
	Marking includes 'closing the gap' comments which allow children to move on in their understanding and use of the language.	
	Lesson observations show that teachers use questioning to assess pupils' understanding, recognising mistakes and misconceptions which are used to facilitate learning.	

Section 6: Leadership and Management

6a: Effectiveness and efficiency of leadership management

Key Question	Evidence	Comments
To what extent does my leadership of modern languages ensure that effective teaching and learning takes place?	The school has an agreed vision of how the implementation is to be planned and carried out.	
	There is a job description and clear line management with records kept of meetings.	
	The Senior Leadership Team is fully supportive and actively promoting languages.	
	Monitoring of lessons and work scrutinies regularly takes place.	
	Governors are fully informed and there is a link governor for languages.	
	Performance management shows the impact on policy and practice.	
	I am aware of the training needs of staff and provide CPD opportunities for them.	
	There is a CPD log and feedback from training undertaken with plans for follow up work.	
	There is a Professional Development Plan, costed over a 3 year period.	
	Financial management records are kept and expenditure is linked to priorities as identified in the subject plan.	
	Input into timetabling to use staff strengths, use of TA support.	
	Minutes are kept of languages meetings where outcomes impact on provision.	
	Monitoring of displays and use of resources ensures that these act as a stimulus for developing the learning.	
	I keep a subject leader log of key issues and reflections.	

Section 7: Overall Effectiveness and Efficiency

Draw together your evaluations in the previous sections to provide an overall statement about the effectiveness of the provision in languages in your school. What are the aspects that are special about languages and of which you feel most proud? Allocate a grade between 1 and 4.

Then state what steps need to be taken to improve the provision further. This can be bullet points. Do not identify more than 3 areas that you plan to work on.

You should also make a statement about the capacity to make further improvement in your area. This can include reference to, for example, a more skilled staff, the success of the monitoring procedures in place, appointment of new staff.

All of the documentation and evidence mentioned should be filed into a Modern Languages Subject Leader File. Having completed your self evaluation, you will be prepared for the visit of the OFSTED Inspector.

» An OFSTED Inspection

Primary languages inspections are part of OFSTED's programme of looking at aspects of the curriculum. An overview of the strengths and weaknesses are published each year with full subject reports every three years.

It is the policy that two weeks' notice will be given to the school but the authors know that in some cases schools have been given only 5 day's notice. It is best if you have your SEF and all documentation ready and not rely on receiving the phone call with enough notice to finish your preparations. The report will be published on the OFSTED website in the usual way. The inspection will last one day. Opposite is an example of one inspection showing the programme for the day and the issues to be addressed.

» Monitoring lessons

The authors maintain that some of the best and most innovative lessons in a primary school will be good language lessons. They will present models of good learning and teaching that can bring real 'excellence and enjoyment' to the primary curriculum. Head teachers and subject leaders have asked how they can judge a good primary languages lesson. Earlier in this book, the characteristics of good language learning have been discussed.

The authors drew on the experience of a European study visit to work with colleagues from Hungary, France and Portugal to isolate the key factors of teacher activity primary languages lesson. A draft monitoring sheet was drawn up and trialled with primary teachers and teaching assistants to produce a criteria shown below. The sheet has been regularly used by Head teachers and Local Authority advisers in monitoring lessons.

One day primary languages inspection key issues to be explored
- How effectively is the school planning and delivering languages?
- The leadership and management regarding the implementation of language entitlement.
- Pupil achievement at the end of Year 6.
- Professional development of staff.
- How is the school assessing achievement and building on it?
- Links with international work.

Timetable of day

8.30 am	Arrive and set up in base room
8.45 am	Meet with Head teacher
9.30 am	Meet with PML Subject Leader
10.00 am	Meet with CPD Co-ordinator
10.30 am	Meet with Chair of GB Curriculum Committee
11.00 am	Lesson observation
11.50 am	Meet with Year 5 and 6 pupils
12.15 pm	Meet with Year 3 and 4 pupils
12.35 pm	Lunch in dining hall with Year 3, 4, 5, 6 pupils
1.00 pm	Scrutiny of documentation
1.35 pm	Lesson observation
2.15 pm	Meet with ICT subject leader
2.40 pm	Scrutiny of documentation and preparation of feedback
4.00 pm	Feedback to Head teacher, Deputy Head teacher, and Primary language subject leader

The primary classroom is the ideal place to learn languages. The approach in every lesson is to use visual, auditory and kinaesthetic support, to be interactive and transactional engaging the interest of all pupils. Criteria for good practice in any subject will apply equally to languages, for example, use of an effective starter, sharing of the lesson objectives and the reviewing and fixing of learning in a plenary.

This checklist of characteristics of a good primary language lesson may be helpful when you are observing lessons and giving feedback to the teacher. Clearly, not all of these may be present in every lesson.

It may be that your school has a generic lesson observation sheet which is used for all subjects and you may have to follow the school format, adding some additional elements for languages.

Characteristics
The teacher radiates enthusiasm and demonstrates that she/he is happy to be there.
There is a good relationship between teacher and pupils and pupils to pupils. Appropriate praise is given and a supportive atmosphere is created where risks can be taken. Good use is made of pupil 'experts'.
There are plenty of opportunities for pupils to use their knowledge of language. The balance between teacher and pupil talk should be at least 60/40, although not necessarily in the new language. Opportunities are provided to talk about the language being learnt. For example, after learning the different greetings provide opportunities to discuss these with the children (see Knowledge about Language strand).
New learning is usually introduced aurally, with visual prompts, mime or other support before the written word is displayed. In some circumstances the teacher may want to present new language in other ways.
The key skills which are emphasised from early on are speaking and listening with reading and writing gaining in importance as pupils become more competent.
Basic instructions are given in the target language as much as possible throughout the lesson. Teachers provide good models of language, either themselves or with the use of video and audio material.
Extensive use is made of visual, auditory and kinaesthetic prompts, clues and activities. Games, songs, puppets and movement are often used. Pupils are fully engaged and are enjoying themselves. Displays of material and pupils' work support learning.
There are plenty of opportunities to hear and repeat new language several times.
A variety of groups is used: whole class, pairs and individuals. At times small groups may also be formed, as appropriate for the task.

As many as possible of the five strands of the Key Stage 2 Framework for languages are incorporated into each lesson appropriate to the context of that lesson and opportunities to talk about language learning strategies are regularly provided.

» Financial monitoring

The monitoring of your finance will be an ongoing task. You will need to keep a record of money spent and how it meets the needs of your curriculum. Ensure that funding is allocated to staff training as well as to resources. This should all be included in your detailed planning, including the Professional Development Plan.

Chapter 6
» Assessment

You may feel that you are too busy just trying to implement languages in your school to be able to spend the time assessing pupils too. This attitude has been picked up in OFSTED subject inspections. However, it is essential that your pupils make the best progress possible and that you and the teachers in your school know how to support them in their learning in the most effective way. In the document 'The Assessment for Learning Strategy' the aims of assessment for learning are set out:

> *'Every child knows how they are doing and understands what they need to do to improve and how to get there. They get the support they need to be motivated, independent learners on an ambitious trajectory of improvement'*
>
> *The Assessment for Learning Strategy*, p4, 2008
> (reference 00341-2008DOM-EN available on **www.teachernet.gov.uk/publication**)

The document goes on to state what are the aims for teachers, schools and parents, and puts forward on p6 three linked aspects of assessment: day to day, periodic and transitional which provide a useful viewpoint. These are aims that teachers want for their pupils in the languages classroom too.

Day to Day	Learning objectives made explicit and shared with pupils Peer and self-assessment in use Pupils engaged in their learning and given immediate feedback
Periodic	Broader view of progress across subject for teacher and learner Use of national standards in the classroom Improvement to medium-term curriculum planning
Transitional	Formal recognition of pupils' achievement Reported to parents/carers and next teachers Uses external tests or tasks

In the excellent book by Jones and Coffey (David Fulton, 2006) on p106, they give examples of assessment techniques. These are shown below.

Application of assessment	Practical examples
Peer assessment	One-to-one peer assessment of speaking, writing or drawing in response to a target language stimulus
	Two stars and a wish
	Group peer review of a spoken effort, e.g. Role-play or a walkie-talkie phone conversation between two pupils
	Peer assessment of audio or video-taped pupil efforts
	Stop and swap work
Self-assessment	Quick recap 'test yourself'
	Self-assessment of taped oral work
	Critical review of written attempt against shared criteria
	Portfolio collection of selected good work or, e.g. Personal CD-ROM folio
	Assessment of progress over time, e.g. tick lists, comments and targets
	Traffic lighting to indicate understanding
	Thumbs up, across or down for same purpose
Pupil reflexivity	Extended wait time
	'Stop and think' spots in lessons
	Pupil learning diary activities
	Problem-solving skills approach, e.g. setting a language learning challenge for the lesson
	Class reflection
	Mind mapping TM/spider diagram techniques
	Traffic lighting own work e.g. with coloured pencils, with coloured sticky dots etc.
	Thinking homework/independent learning task

Application of assessment	Practical examples
Teacher assessment that is compatible	Two stars and a wish
	Competitions, songs and games with an assessment aim
	Listen and point/mime/tick
	Read and draw
	Qualitative comments and targets

» Day to day assessments

From Year 3 onwards you will want to start assessing your pupils' achievements so that you can be informed about their progress and to help them in making the next steps in their language learning journey. As the planning and the teaching are objectives driven and based on the requirements of the Key Stage 2 Framework, the first point about the learning objectives being explicit and shared with pupils will not be difficult to deal with as primary practitioners. You will want to observe how well pupils are achieving the objectives and in what areas they need further support. Your dynamic teaching will ensure that the pupils are engaged. You will give them immediate verbal feedback which can be just simple praise or questioning to extend them further. For example you can involve them in simple self assessment. This can be just a thumb-up-thumbs-down response to role-play. Or you can give each pupil a 'traffic light' of red, yellow and green cards. These can be used to give feedback to the teacher where they can be used as part of the plenary for the teacher to pick out which pupils are having difficulty. This can then inform the immediate planning where certain ideas and concepts that several children have not fully grasped, where they have responded with a yellow card, can be subsequently revisited.

In addition to assessing the development of language skills, knowledge and understanding, you will want your teachers to make a note of pupils':
- growing confidence;
- independence;
- enjoyment;
- collaboration with others;
- language learning strategies;
- ability to be creative;
- ability to be reflective and to evaluate their own learning.

In order to assess appropriately, it is vital to understand the Key Stage 2 Framework strands. Within each strand are levels of progression which the subject leader is able to recognise in children's linguistic development. There is support in progression in two documents: The Key Stage 2 Framework, Part 3 and the Teacher's Guide for the QCA

Schemes of Work for French, German and Spanish. Both documents describe progression in the five strands.

In the QCA Scheme of Work *Teacher's Guide* (2007), Appendix 1: Progression in early language learning, for example, there are suggested way in which progression in language skills and language-learning skills might be developed (see p26). On p5 of the same document, in a discussion on Oracy it is stated that 'In the early stages of language learning, children spend much of their time listening and speaking'. You will want them to have accurate pronunciation and intonation. There will, therefore, be many things to take into consideration when assessing pupils' progress.

» Self-Assessment using the European Language Portfolio – Junior Version

The purpose of this European Language Portfolio is for pupils to record their own experience of all languages. This means that it should include achievements and skills in a range of languages, not just the one being taught in school. It belongs to the pupil and is designed to be used as a record of achievements around positive 'can-do' statements. The portfolio is available from CILT with a Teacher's Guide showing how best it can be used. It can also be downloaded from the Primary Languages website.

The portfolio contains:
- a language passport where pupils record their language-learning experiences;
- a language biography which is like a learning diary where pupils can colour in speech bubbles of can-do statements in the four language skills;
- a self-assessment section where the pupils evaluate how they are 'getting better';
- a personal dossier which is rather like a 'good work folder' to keep pieces of work which pupils choose for themselves.

» The Languages Ladder

This is a scheme to measure progress and make sense of the claim that people can get credit for their language learning at whatever age. There are 17 grades arranged across 6 stages from Breakthrough to Mastery. The nationally expected level that primary pupils will achieve after four years of learning a language is grade 3 Breakthrough. But pupils may progress to grade 4 in, for example, speaking. Each skill may be assessed discretely. The level of performance in each skill is defined by 'can-do' statements. Pupils do not need to be at the same grade in each skill.

What you want staff to do over the course of Year 3, for example, is to 'catch' pupils saying short phrases or words really well. Look back at Chapter 2 where there is a discussion on promoting excellent teaching to remind you and your staff what you are looking for when assessing good language learning. Also, if you can, encourage teachers to talk to the Foundation Stage staff about observing and assessing pupil learning.

Now put a large poster on your wall with the speaking (and possibly listening grades) from the Languages Ladder displayed. The rest of the poster will be blank. Example poster below:

> **Speaking Grade 1 – I can say/repeat a few words and short simple phrases**
>
> **Grade 2 – I can answer simple questions and give basic information.**

When you catch pupils saying a few words or answering questions then make a note, date it, write the name of the child and stick it on your poster. It gives you the opportunity to record unexpected and surprising contributions too. Every few weeks you may like to target 6 children in particular to make the process manageable and to give focus to your assessment. Many teachers keep notes in a type of mark book and build up a picture of each pupil's progress in the four language skills over the year. Probably you will not start this recording until the second half of the Autumn Term. Ideally, you will be the class teacher as well as the languages teacher so can take opportunities throughout the week to make assessments and to focus on particular children. Ensure that you give each child the opportunity to be assessed in this way several times over the year.

Also, set up a computer in each classroom with a microphone where pupils' speaking can be captured. For this you can use **www.download-audacity.com** You can use these recorded pieces to get pupils to listen to themselves and to suggest ways that they might improve their accent or intonation. This can also be used for peer assessment.

In addition, you may want to create a chart using the list on pp26 and 27 in the QCA Teacher's Guide as a starting point to record what each child can do. You can use signs and phrases around the wall as items for the pupils to read and respond to. The can involve reading aloud so that you can gauge how well pupils are progressing in matching the sounds with the spelling of words.

» Periodic and Transitional Assessment

In the Chapter on Transition and Transfer the authors give an example of a Year 6 reporting form which can be used as a transition document to inform secondary schools of the level of attainment of each pupil. It combines teacher and pupil self-assessment against the Languages Ladder grades and aspects of language learning skills and knowledge about language. The nationally expected level after four years of language learning is Grade 3. To record periodic assessment of speaking and listening, the following format is suggested as an example.

(Tick appropriate box)

Name: Pupil 1/Pupil 2	Pupil 1	Pupil 2
Context: (For example a role play using greetings and asking for and giving personal information) The pupil can:		
Understand a range of familiar spoken phrases (Level 2)	☐	☐
Say a few words and short simple phrases (Level 1)	☐	☐
Answer simple questions and give basic information (Level 2)	☐	☐
Speak with a good accent (Level 2)	☐	☐
Be understood but need to improve accent (Level 1)	☐	☐
Speak with good intonation (Level 2)	☐	☐
Be understood but needs to improve rhythm of speech (Level 1)	☐	☐
Speak with confidence and expression (Level 2)	☐	☐
Speak hesitantly (Level 1)	☐	☐
Overall level of speaking	☐	☐
Overall level of listening	☐	☐

Signature	Date

Another way of gaining evidence of your pupils' level of attainment would be to use some of the materials produced by the OCR Examinations Board for the Asset Languages or indeed to enter them for the Asset Languages qualification.

» Asset Languages

'Asset Languages is a way of recognising and rewarding achievement in languages learning from OCR. The Asset Languages assessment scheme supports the government's National Languages Strategy and is designed to provide voluntary accreditation options for learners of all ages and abilities from primary to further, higher and adult education'

www.assetlanguages.org.uk

The first stage is the Breakthrough Stage at which point the pupil will have reached grade 3. This is the first stage at which external assessment for OCR qualifications are offered. Before that there is teacher assessment for grades 1 and 2.

Chapter 7
» Your own school community and beyond

In this chapter you will find out how to make the most of international links and projects as well as advice on promoting languages in your school and community.

» International projects and links

The subject leader's main purpose is to ensure that the pupils have a high quality language experience that sets them on the road to becoming able, creative linguists. The role of the teacher is key to this process. Ensure that you take advantage of all the opportunities that are available to meet your own needs, as well as supporting the other staff at your school. A major way to learn with time to stand back from your daily hurly-burly and look at things afresh is to take part in international visits.

You should contact your Local Authority to find out what support they can provide.

Any international link enhances and provides opportunities for learning about each other's language and cultural traditions.

> 'We live in one world. What we do affects others and what
> others do affects us, as never before. To recognise that we
> are all members of a world community and that we all have
> responsibilities to each other is not romantic rhetoric, but
> modern economic and social reality'
>
> (*Putting the world into class education*, p9, DfES 2004).

Schools are expected to have an international link by 2012.

As the subject leader you will be able to pursue many options. Here are some ideas of suitable programmes. International visits can be an excellent way of getting staff on board. Also a link with a partner school which speaks the language you teach can act as a catalyst to developing your work.

» Comenius school-based projects

These projects will provide many occasions to share experiences with pupils in other countries. For example, the project 'A day in the life of pupils in different countries' enables children to study the similarities and differences of pupils' lives providing many cross curricular links. This study naturally encompasses the objectives in the International Understanding strand of the Framework for Languages. It can also help to cover the literacy strand objectives when the children exchange, for example, emails, letters or cards. This is even more relevant where the language studied is spoken by one of the partner schools.

Suggested activities as part of the project:
- Daily timetables, including the length of the school day.
- School life.
- Home life.
- Leisure activities.
- Families.
- Types of food.
- Pets.
- Clothes.
- School sports.
- Methods of transport.
- Playground games.

The opportunity for pupils to travel to their link schools is now a feature of the Comenius projects. For example, Hazelbury Junior School took their steel pan band to visit and perform at a school near Tours as part of their project 'United by Music'. As the pupils had been studying French, this enabled them to practise the language during the visit and try out their skills in their partner school.

Projects can also contribute to the development of interpersonal skills. In the Hadley Wood project, communication between pupils of different nationalities was a prominent feature. One of the outcomes of the project was the production of phrase books in French and Italian to support the pupils in all three countries in communicating with each other. This gave pupils confidence to write about themselves, as the following letter shows.

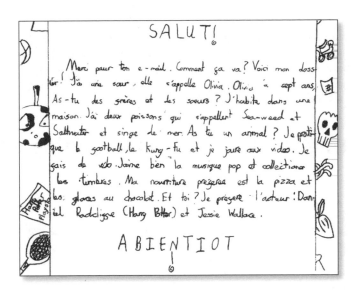

» Joint Curriculum Projects

These projects involve pupil mobility. For example 36 pupils from 4 Enfield schools travelled to Gerleve in Germany for 6 days to work on a joint project 'Festivals' with their link school, Lambertischule. During their visit the children took part in the local Karneval celebrations, shared their ideas and experiences of festivals and studied different festivals, for example Diwali, Eid, Christmas in groups. They made masks and wore them in the festival procession to mark Rose Monday

It is a wet day at the Karneval in Coesfeld, North Germany. The Enfield pupils and teachers sport wigs!

There is a wide variety of international, including European, projects which schools can access. For further details go to the British Council website **www.britishcouncil.org** or to **www.globalgateways.org** where you will find detailed information on the content of the programmes, with case studies, plus full details of all international opportunities managed by the British Council.

» Promoting the subject – maintaining a high profile

Again, you will have to be more proactive than others in school in promoting the subject to allay some of the possible concerns. It is important to maintain a high profile for the language teaching and this can be achieved in many ways.

» Assemblies

Encourage teachers to use their class assembly to share the children's language learning with the rest of the school. The pupils can perform simple rhymes and songs or role plays which reflect their language experiences. Draw up a rota for whole-school assemblies with a language focus. Parents and governors should be invited to these assemblies to give the learning a high profile.

» European Day of Languages

The European Day of Languages (EDL), a Council of Europe initiative, is held annually on the 26 September to celebrate language and cultural diversity. The Day was first celebrated in 2001, the European Year of Languages and involves more people every year. It is:
- a Europe-wide celebration of all the world's languages;
- a day to kick-start language learning;
- a chance to raise awareness about the value of language skills.

and aims to:
- alert the public to the importance of language learning;
- increase awareness and appreciation of all languages;
- encourage lifelong language learning.

Most events and activities are held on the day itself, but some people extend the celebrations over two or three days and others even have a whole week of language-related events. Whether you decide on a single activity or a series of events, there are a range of resources to help you make the day special.

View the Council of Europe Events calendar at **www.ecml.at/edl/find.asp?s=EV** to see what took place on the European Day of Languages 2008. If you are planning a languages celebration of your own then don't forget to add your own event, even if it is not open to the public.

Pupils take part in European Day of Languages 2008

Pupils carry flags in a special EDL 2008 assembly

» Newsletters

Most schools communicate the school's events to parents via regular newsletters. Ensure that you submit articles to inform parents of the latest developments on languages in your school.

» Language activities week

Agree with your Senior Leadership Team that one week a year is designated as a language week covering as much of the curriculum as possible.

» Suggestions for the organisation of a French week

PE

- Play games of *boules* use coloured mats or cones or hoops to practise colours or numbers. Use *Take 10 en français*.
- Play *Jacques a dit* (Simon says).

History

- Celebrate Bastille Day (July 14th).
- Find out about the life of Jeanne d'Arc.
- Find pictures on the internet of the Bayeaux tapestry and investigate its background.

- Act the meeting of Henry VIII and Francis 1st at the Field of the Cloth of Gold (*le camp du drap d'or*) near Arras in the North of France.
- Carry out a project on Napoléon and Joséphine.

Music

- Teach the children a regional folk dance from Brittany, Provence or the Basque country.
- Use the music from Le Carnaval des animaux by Saint-Saens.

Art

- Compare famous French painters such as the Impressionist painters and paint pictures in the style of one of the painters.
- Look at images of modern French architecture e.g. the glass pyramids in front of the Louvre and the Pompidou centre with its coloured pipes.
- Carry out a project on the Eiffel Tower, its history, its structure, its measurement and create models of the Eiffel Tower in different media.

Literature

- Read stories aloud, such as the Hungry Caterpillar in French
- Create similar stories using ICT.
- Look at comic books such as Astérix and Tintin and ask the children to create new characters.

Drama

- Put on a small play
- Organise a series of role plays created and acted by pupils reflecting their current learning in the language.

ICT

- Create a leaflet on Paris.
- Consult websites recommended.

Geography

- Produce and deliver a weather forecast using props.

Maths

- Carry out short daily mental maths activities
- Sing number songs on the Français, Français tape.
- Textiles
- Embroider a French word onto a bookmark or mat made from binca.

Technology

- Create a board game
- Make a model of a French monument or of the guillotine.

Home Economics
- Introduce the children to French food (samples of the food can be tasted and opinions given on them with evaluation sheets)
- Have a French breakfast and carry out a survey 'j'aime, je n'aime pas'.

General Activities
- Run a shopping experience with real French items using Euros, with a passport and French activities
- Dress up in French colours for a day.
- Dress up as French characters.
- Organise a photo competition of French objects or food.

» Class language of the year

Allocate each class a different language of the year (in addition to your main school language). The class teacher and pupils over the course of the year have to learn some key phrases in that language; decide on one country where that language is spoken and find out as much as they can about it; invite in, if possible, native speakers of that language to talk about their lives and to tell stories.

» Language of the month

If you prefer to have a whole-school approach then each month choose a different language which may reflect on the make-up of your school population and all useful phrases for a central school display. The Newbury Park School website **www.newburypark.redbridge.sch.uk/langofmonth/index.html** has loads of ideas.

» Using interactive displays

To reinforce learning you should help to set up a language corner in every classroom. This might involve:
- A poster relevant to the current learning, for example, parts of the body, which gives the opportunity for the teacher to pose questions to individual pupils during the week.
- A table with dual language and foreign language readers and non-fictional books.
- Artefacts with separate labels which individual pupils can have the opportunity to match up to the object.
- Samples of pupils' work, photos, items to highlight cultural aspects.
- Displays of common words and phrases in use every day, for example, days of the week, months, weather.

• Language specific to the units of work being studied, displayed with vibrant colourful material to highlight the phrases.

» Communicating and involving parents

The annual report to parents should include information on achievement in languages. Parents need to be fully involved and informed.

Hold meetings to explain the programme to parents and to audit their language skills.

This is an example of a letter which could be sent to parents inviting them to an after school meeting.

Ashwood School
Acacia Road
Sycamore Av.
United Kingdom
AB12 C34

Dear Parents/carers

You have no doubt heard that the teaching of foreign languages will be a requirement for all schools with children in Key Stage 2 by September 2010.

Your child will be involved from _____ .

We are keen to inform you about what will happen in the classroom and to gain your support to help your child succeed. You may have some questions for us and these will all be dealt with at the meeting. We as a school are very excited about this new addition to the curriculum and brings England in line with the majority of countries in Europe. We know that you will be interested to know how you can be part of this development.

Please come along to the meeting on __/__/__

Yours truly

If appropriate, at the meeting you may ask some pupils to make a presentation and demonstrate their learning to date, even if your language teaching is at an early stage. It is always impressive to see how quickly children have acquired some basic skills and to see how much they are enjoying the learning. You will also want to find out what language skills parents have in order to draw on these to support language events in the school.

Here is a sample questionnaire that you may ask parents to complete.

Questionnaire

1. Do you speak any languages in addition to English?

Yes ☐ No ☐

2. If yes, please state which language(s)

....

....

3. How confident are you in speaking the language(s)?

1 ☐ 2 ☐ 3 ☐ 4 ☐

Where 1 = basic and 4 = fluent

4. Would you be interested in helping to support language events?

Yes ☐ No ☐

5. Any other comments

....

....

....

....

....

....

Galliard Primary school sent a questionnaire to the parents of Year 3 pupils after they had begun to implement the teaching of German. Here is an example of one of the feedback sheets from a parent.

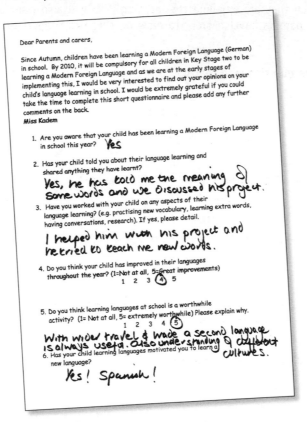

Dear Parents and carers,

Since Autumn, children have been learning a Modern Foreign Language (German) in school. By 2010, it will be compulsory for all children in Key Stage two to be learning a Modern Foreign Language and as we are at the early stages of implementing this, I would be very interested to find out your opinions on your child's language learning in school. I would be extremely grateful if you could take the time to complete this short questionnaire and please add any further comments on the back.

Miss Kadem

1. Are you aware that your child has been learning a Modern Foreign Language in school this year? **Yes**

2. Has your child told you about their language learning and shared anything they have learnt?
   Yes, he has told me the meaning of some words and we discussed his project.

3. Have you worked with your child on any aspects of their language learning? (e.g. practising new vocabulary, learning extra words, having conversations, research). If yes, please detail.
   I helped him with his project and he tried to teach me new words.

4. Do you think your child has improved in their languages throughout the year? (1=Not at all, 5=Great improvements)
   1 2 3 ④ 5

5. Do you think learning languages at school is a worthwhile activity? (1= Not at all, 5= extremely worthwhile) Please explain why.
   1 2 3 4 ⑤
   With wider travel & trade a second language is always useful. Also understanding of different cultures.

6. Has your child learning languages motivated you to learn a new language?
   Yes! Spanish!

» Accessing and managing external support

The subject leaders should make all staff aware of the external support and courses available. It is vital for the subject leader to manage the support received by the school and to be clear about exactly what support they wish to be provided. One source of support may be specialist language teachers or consultants who come into your school. In many local authorities support is provided by a Language College. The relationship needs to be managed throughout. The following suggestions show ways in which the role of a visiting teacher can be managed:

- Invite the teacher to the school for the day and invite her/him to sit in on classes to become acquainted with the primary curriculum.
- Introduce the teacher to all staff members.
- During lessons make sure that the class teacher stays in the classroom and is involved in the lesson.

- Ensure that the class teacher is given the plans of the lesson.
- Ensure that there are opportunities for daily follow up to the lesson.
- Arrange for time for the class teacher and the visiting teacher to talk after the lesson.
- Provide the opportunity for communications between lessons, for example, emails, phone calls.

The following is an example of the contract that we use for schools and visiting language specialists.

KS2 Languages Support Agreement

Name of host school: ……………………………………………..

Headteacher: ………………………………………………..

As part of the work to embed language teaching across KS1 I agree that:

– The teacher will remain in the class whilst the language lesson is delivered and will join in enthusiastically.

– The support teacher will be informed well in advance using their contact details below if it is not possible to hold the lesson on the agreed date.

– Planning time after the lesson will be provided.

– I will send a teacher on the KS2 training sessions.

Signed: ……………………………………………………………

Date: ……………………………………………………………

****

Name of support teacher: ……………………………………………...

Contact details: ……………………………………………………

I will always keep to the agreement to teach in the host school on the dates agreed and will turn up in advance of the lesson.

I understand that this primary languages time has priority over my own school events.

I will carry out the tasks, as detailed overleaf.

Signed: …………………………………………………………

Date: …………………………………………………………

Page 1 of 2

Role of the support teacher

1. Before the lesson

- To plan the lessons.

2. During the lesson

- To model good practice and engage the pupils.

- To involve the other adults in the room and work to get them to contribute progressively more and more to the lesson.

3. After the lesson

- To discuss with staff the key learning points.

- To plan with the staff how they are going to reinforce the learning over the next week.

- To leave written ideas with the teachers on how in the subsequent lesson pupils can practise and recap the learning.

Page 2 of 2

Chapter 8
» Transition and transfer

The role of the subject leader is crucial in establishing and maintaining effective transition links and communication between primary and secondary schools. You will need to work in partnership with your link schools to ensure that continuity in language learning is ensured and that pupils' progress is recognised.

The following advice is intended to help you to draw up your school's plans to deal with the diverse aspects of transition in your subject area. Extensive helpful guidance on the subject of transition is also found in Part 3, Section 6, of the Framework of Languages.

Research carried out for the DCSF on transition *The Impact of School Transitions* and *Transfer on Pupil Progress and Attainment*, in 1999. The document does not cover language specifically, but did come up with the notion of five transition bridges.

» The five transition bridges

1 **Administrative bridge** – sharing information about pupils, good working relationships between primary and secondary schools, feedback to primary schools of Year 7 progress.
2 **Social and Personal bridge** – induction days, open evenings, pupil peer mentoring, pupil and parents guides.
3 **Curriculum bridge** – effective use of pupil data, cross-phrase projects, exchange of curriculum maps, joint planning.
4 **Pedagogical bridge** – shared understanding of effective teaching and learning, team teaching, teacher exchanges.
5 **Management of Learning bridge** – pupils are active participants in transition and their own learning, pupil portfolio.

We suggest activities below which go some way to fulfilling the building bricks identified in the five transition bridges.

» Creating the link

Establish whether there exists a whole school transition policy or procedures and what links are already in place between your primary school and link secondary schools on which you can build.

Arrange for an initial informal meeting with the language teachers in the secondary school as a bridge to establishing network meetings.

» Network meetings

These meetings will enable you to work together with your primary and secondary colleagues on the issues involved in transition. The following are areas for consideration in these meetings:

- Share experiences with other primary schools in your area.
- Ensure that there is regular contact between primary and secondary teachers.
- Invite secondary teachers in to your school to see a range of lessons across the curriculum to familiarise them with primary methodology.
- Arrange for Year 7 teachers to observe language lessons in your school. This will give them an opportunity to know the language teaching skills which have been developed in primary schools and how the emphasis is on the cross-curricular approach. The secondary teachers will be happy to take part in lessons and share their skills. There will be greater benefit if you have the opportunity to have discussions prior to and after the lessons.
- Arrange for primary teachers to observe Year 7 lessons so that they have an understanding of the level of skills expected of their pupils in Key Stage 3 and of the Key Stage 3 curriculum. This contact should enable your primary language teachers to appreciate the impact on Key Stage 3 of the introduction of language learning in the primary curriculum. It will give you, as subject leader, knowledge of the KS3 objectives and of the cross-curricular approach which is now at the heart of the KS3 curriculum.
- Suggest that staff from the different Key Stages have joint training days in which they try different language activities and methodology with a focus on transferable skills and core competencies. Plan to set up common training sessions with your secondary colleagues.
- Try to arrange as much contact as possible between pupils and staff in the Key stages. Year 6 pupils could act as pupil ambassadors by visiting Year 7 classes to share their understanding and skills. They may perform role plays, take part in conversations and show their portfolios. Year 7 pupils could visit Year 6 classes to act as leaders. These visits could be arranged to take place in regular lessons. In some authorities secondary pupils are now supporting

the teaching of languages in Year 3 which has had an impact on their own learning and on their social skills.

- Other special days could be a point of contact for pupils and teachers. You could invite secondary teachers and pupils to share in any celebrations at your school and arrange to visit events organised by the secondary schools. These might range from celebrating the European Day of Languages on 26th September, inset days, language festivals, assemblies, language themed days and cultural events. It might be possible to arrange to set up joint activities to cement the links between the primary and secondary schools which could involve pupils, teachers, parents, governors, the LA.

- The meetings would provide a forum for sharing information on wider issues. These would include information on any contact with partners abroad, such as the Comenius projects, ventures such as the Joint Curriculum Projects and any links with the local community.

- The possibility for sharing policies, teaching and learning materials, resources in general and ICT resources in particular should be discussed at these meetings.

» Cross phase projects

The Primary Strategy has developed bridging units in English which begin in Year 6 and are completed in Year 7. The aim is to provide pupils with a unit of work which crosses the primary-secondary divide and allows them to demonstrate key skills. On the Enfield MFL website there is a cross-phase project in Spanish based on the QCA Unit 24 which gives pupils the opportunity to consolidate their learning drawing on the work covered in KS2 **www.mfl.enfield.lgfl.net**. It starts in Year 6 and continues into Year 7 providing a starting point which the secondary teacher can build on. The Year 7 teacher will gain a real idea of the level of each pupil's skills.

There are also materials on transition and transfer on the CILT website at **www.cilt.org.uk**.

» Transfer of information

As subject leader you will be responsible for data management. You will need to share information with colleagues in Key Stage 3 so that pupils' progress in language learning can be recognised and tracked from Key Stage 2 to Key Stage 3. You may already have been using the Languages Ladder which has been developed to help teachers to record and track pupil progress. This is discussed in more length in Chapter 6. Through the use of the Languages Ladder you can assess your pupils' achievements in the different levels. This information can be used to produce a transition document or report on each pupil. This document will then outline the children's levels in Listening, Speaking, Reading and Writing and should contain information about Knowledge about Language and Language Learning Strategies used by the pupils. It is crucial that there is some recognition of the good habits that have been fostered in primary schools, using the KS2 Objectives as the guide.

Pupils have developed strategies to help them learn languages and have used their knowledge of a variety of languages to explore language structures. There should be room on the transition document for pupil assessment. In addition, if pupils complete their own personal details this will make the process more manageable for the Year 6 teachers.

Below is an example which we has been used in a number of North London boroughs. It has been kept short and relatively simple to assist the Year 7 teachers.

Key Stage 2 Languages Report

Primary School: _____

Name of Pupil: _____

Language(s): _____

Number of Years of study: _____ Approximate time per week: _____

Secondary School Attending: _____

The pupil has reached the following grades on the Language Ladder

Listening: _____ Speaking: _____

Reading: _____ Writing: _____

She/he can: Please tick one box for each as appropriate	Fully	Partially	Not yet
Manipulate language	☐	☐	☐
Understand and use negatives	☐	☐	☐
Notice and match agreements	☐	☐	☐
Use knowledge of word order to construct sentences	☐	☐	☐

She/he can: Please tick one box for each as appropriate	Fully	Partially	Not yet
Use a dictionary	☐	☐	☐
Discuss how language is learnt	☐	☐	☐
Has strategies to help remember phrases	☐	☐	☐
Pronounce phrases correctly	☐	☐	☐

Pupil comment on learning languages:

Things I am good at: _____

My best memory is: _____

Other languages I speak: _____

It may be that the language studied in your school will not be the same as that studied in Key Stage 3. In that case, the information given in the languages report on transferable language skills and knowledge about language and how it works, is particular important.

» European Language Portfolio

In addition, you may already have been using the European Language Portfolio in which your children will have been recording their own achievements and language experiences. This portfolio will provide a picture for your secondary colleagues of the skill, understanding and enthusiasm of the individual pupils especially as it will contain personal items such as photos, examples of work and comments by the pupils.

Results of formal assessments such as Asset Languages will be passed on to the link schools. These assessments have been discussed more fully in Chapter 6.

» Key Stage 1 transfer

The preceding advice has, of course, been based on the transition arrangements from KS2 to KS3. Although there is no statutory requirement for languages to be studied at KS1 it is acknowledged in the Framework for Languages that the introduction of languages at this stage can be very beneficial and indeed may well be established in your own school. In Part 3, Section 3 of the Framework for Languages, advice is given on the transition from KS1 to KS2 as well as on the methodology for languages in KS1. This shows how the more informal approach for KS1 teaching can form a basis for more formal teaching of the language in KS2.

» Key Stage 3 curriculum

There are now exciting developments in the Key Stage 3 curriculum providing strong links with what is already happening in the Key Stage 2 curriculum. The overarching themes are similar, being based on cross-curricular approach to language learning.

The programme of study for KS3 **www.qca.org.uk/curriculum** shows that the Key concepts and Key Processes lead on naturally from those outlined in the Framework for Languages for Key Stage 2.

Key Concepts for KS3:
  1.1 Linguistic competence
  1.2 Knowledge about language
  1.3 Creativity
  1.4 Intercultural understanding

Key Processes for KS3:
  2.1 Developing language learning strategies
  2.2 Developing language skills

It will be useful for you to visit the QCA website shown above. It can be seen that the concepts and processes are in many ways very similar to those for Key Stage 2, although, of course, they extend and challenge pupils in KS3.

Under the section for Curriculum Opportunities the importance is now stressed of establishing links with English, ICT and other subjects as is already the case for Key Stage 2. It emphasises how important it is to 'use the target language in connection with topics and issues that are engaging and may be related to other areas of the curriculum.' The revised KS3 objectives will ensure that there is easier progression from KS2 to KS3.

» Conclusion

The authors hope that they have helped you to start on the road to becoming a successful languages subject leader. The aim of this book has been to help guide you through the many aspects of this important post. As long as you have the support of your Head teacher and the Governing Body, you will be able to implement languages within the primary curriculum following the advice and ideas contained in this book. We wish you the best of luck and congratulate you on making the decision to take on this challenge.

» Bibliography

CILT ELL DVD

CILT Young Pathfinder 11: *A Flying Start!* June de Silva and Peter Satchwell

CILT Young Pathfinder 15: *Speak Up!* Peter Satchwell with June de Silva

Consejería de Educación and Instituto Cervantes. **http://ave.cervantes.es**

DCSF (2008) *Improving Schools Programme* – The Primary Strategy

Devon Education Services (2008) *Take 10 en français*

DFES (1990) *All our Futures*

DFES *Excellence and Enjoyment* 0377/2003. **http://www.standards.d.csf.gov.uk/primary/publications/literacy/63553**

DFES (2007) *Languages Review* 00212 – 2007DOM-EN

DFES (2002) *Languages for All: Languages for Life* DFES/0749/2002

DFES (2005) *Leading and Co-ordinating CPD in Secondary Schools*

DFES 2005 *Leading and Co-ordinating in Secondary Schools*

DFES(2004) *Putting the world into class education*

DFES (2005) *The Key Stage 2 Framework for Languages* 1721-2005DCD-EN

Early Start DVD. **www.earlystart.com**

European Language Portfolio. **www.cilt.org.uk/books/portfolios.htm**

Goethe Institute

Jones and Coffey (2006) *Modern Foreign Languages 5–11*, David Fulton, London.

Joyce B and Showers B (1988) *Student Achievement through staff development*, Longman, London

KS3 Programme of Study. **www.qca.org.uk/curriculum**

KS3 Strategic Learning Networks. **www.cilt.org.uk/KS3/dissemination.htm**

Newbury Park School. **www.newburypark.redbridge.sch.uk/langofmonth/index.html**

Pyne, D (2007) Unpublished MA module: Middlesex University MIDWHEB

QCA (2007) *Scheme of Work Teachers' Guide*

TDA (2007) *Professional Standards for Teachers.***www.tda.gov.uk/standards**

The Assessment for Learning Strategy (2008) 00341-2008DOM-EN.

www.teachernet.gov.uk/publications

TIPD Beijing Report (2006) Enfield

(Transition) 1999

» Useful websites

www.dfes.gov.uk/research/data/uploadfiles/RR131.doc

www.britishcouncil.org/comenius

www.britishcouncil.org.globalschools

www.bbc.co.uk/languages

www.cilt.org.uk

www.cilt.org.uk/KS3/dissemination.htm

www.tda.gov.uk

www.midwheb.org.uk

www.deseducation.org

www.assetlanguages.org.uk

www.teachernet.gov.uk/publications

www.mfl.enfield.lgfl.net

www.globalgateway.org

www.everychildmatters.gov.uk

www.primarylanguages.org.uk

www.languagefactory.com

www.atantot.com